Praying O

PRAYING OUR GOODBYES

Joyce Rupp

eagle

Guildford, Surrey

British Library Cataloguing in Publication Data. A catalogue record for this book is available from the British Library.

Published in the USA by Ave Maria Press. This edition published 1995 in the UK by Eagle, an imprint of Inter Publishing Service (IPS) Ltd, St Nicholas House, 14 The Mount, Guildford, Surrey GU2 5HN.

All Scripture quotations, unless otherwise noted, are taken from *The Jerusalem Bible*. Copyright © 1966 Darton, Longman and Todd Ltd. Used by permission. Scripture quotations labelled:

NIV: *New International Version*

GNB: *Good News Bible*

NAB: *New American Bible*

When Someone We Love from the album *Rise Up*. Copyright © 1983, The Benedictine Foundation of the State of Vermont, Inc.

Lines on page 19 from *The Poetry of Robert Frost* edited by Edward Connery Lathem. Copyright © 1969 Holt, Rinehart and Winston, Inc.

Lines from "Like a Flock of Homesick Cranes" and from "New Melodies Break Forth From the Heart" in GITANJALI by Rabindranath Tagore (New York: Macmillan/Collier Books, 1971).

Typeset by Watermark, Norfolk
Printed at Thomson Press (India) Limited

ISBN 0 86347 154 4

Dedication

To Dad
his wisdom, laughter,
enthusiasm for life
and deep love of the earth
are among my greatest treasures

and

to Emily Palmer, O.S.M.,
Servite sister and friend,
her courage in living
and in dying
has blessed me

Contents

Foreword

Sometimes, when I'm gazing at someone else's shelf-ful of books, one seems to beg to be picked up. *Praying Our Goodbyes* was one such book. I was leading a retreat in New Zealand at the time. A fellow retreatgiver told me that she had brought some of her books with her and that she would be happy for members of the team to borrow them if they so wished. Bookworm that I am, I took the first possible opportunity to browse. I was preparing to say a particularly painful goodbye at the time. That's why, when the book seemed to beckon, I responded.

Taking *Praying Our Goodbyes* from the shelf, I turned first one page, then another. Instinctively, I discerned that I was clutching a gem. I not only borrowed the book for the duration of the retreat. I copied out chunks of it and I asked the friend to whom I was about to say my pain-filled goodbye whether she knew where I could buy my own copy. She found one and gave it to me as a parting gift. Though continents separated us after that, together we used Joyce Rupp's insights as we prayed and grew through that particular goodbye.

The book made such a profound impact on both of us that, when I moved from England to Cyprus, I took it with me. When Mission Partners and others started to come on retreat with us, I found that, over and over again, one of the things they needed to do was to pray a goodbye of one sort or another. Some were suffering the loss of a loved one through death, a mother, a father, a sister, a brother; others were suffering loss of a different kind – the loss of a partner through the break-up of a marriage, the loss of status and identity and job-fulfilment through moving overseas, the loss of seeming security by exchanging a fixed, handsome income for a Mission Partner's meagre stipend. Yet others seemed to be crawling through the tunnel of transition: facing the challenge of saying goodbye to one form of spirituality and exchanging it for another; moving from one of life's phases into another.

Over and over again, I found myself suggesting that an individual should spend part of their retreat reading and praying in the unique insights with which this book is packed. Consequently, over and over again, I was asked the question: 'Where can I buy my own copy?' That is why I found myself longing that this book might form a part of the *Exploring Prayer* series.

David Wavre, Managing Director of Eagle Books, responded to my enthusiastic suggestion by recommending that I should write to Frank Cunningham, Director of Ave Maria Press in America. At first Frank Cunningham was understandably cautious, but, at the same time, courteous and warm in his response. As our correspondence continued, however, the cautiousness seemed to evaporate and, on behalf of the author, he co-operated in the project as fully as he possibly could. I am grateful to him and to David Wavre for their help and am particularly grateful to the author for allowing us to anglicise and slightly abbreviate her original manuscript.

The original book has already been greatly used by God in the USA and New Zealand and I am delighted that it is now to become easily accessible to British readers. I used the book when the time came for my husband and myself to uproot from England and to settle in Cyprus. I used it when my brother died. I use it whenever I am faced with the pain of saying goodbye to those who have come to visit us in Cyprus, for the pain of parting does not decrease with practice I find.

And so, without hesitation, I recommend this book to anyone who is being confronted with the challenge of saying goodbye: to a career maybe, to good health, to a precious relationship, to security of one kind or another. I recommend, too, that when readers are searching for a love gift to give to a Mission Partner about to depart for their new life overseas, or to the relatives or close friends of such a person, they could not do better than to give this book. Or, if you are searching for a book that might help a person grow through the trauma of loss of whatever kind, that you might consider giving them this book that will be to them the friend they need to help them make sense of a painful transition.

Joyce Huggett
Cyprus
June 1995

Introduction

It was 1968. I had never thought about anyone in my family dying. I was young and they all seemed so full of life. Then came the phone call and my sister's voice saying, 'I am so sorry to have to be the one to tell you. We lost Dave today. . . .' My 23-year-old brother, the one next in age to me, had drowned. Dave was the one I dearly loved and had yearned to know better. The memory of our last time together flashed through my mind: Dave, sitting in the easy chair smiling at me, and I, feeling a kind of sadness because we had so much yet to learn and to share with one another. Our time together had seemed all too short. Strange how I remember the exact words and know precisely what I was doing at the exact moment when the phone rang. The shock of that message deeply embedded the details in my memory.

The painful truth of how hard it is to say goodbye started to root itself and take hold in my heart. As I look back, I feel as though I have had this book in my soul for a long, long time. While it is a book about farewell to our loved ones who have died, it is also about many other forms of goodbye in our lives, all those events and experiences in which we feel a deep sense of loss. I believe that instead of running from these goodbyes, we need to take the time to reflect upon them, to 'pray them'. In doing so we can become wiser, deeper and more compassionate.

Although life is difficult and always has its share of sorrows, life is also very good and deeply enriching. It holds many promises of growth and treasures of joy. It is not easy to believe this when we are hurting greatly because of our loss. Sometimes it takes years to understand and accept this truth. That is how it has been for me.

The grief of losing my brother touched numerous areas of my life. I found myself fighting, avoiding, struggling with and being angry or confused about the many forms of goodbye that I experienced: being uprooted from one place to another, deaths of family friends and a dear uncle, termination of a significant friendship of many years, betrayal by one I had really trusted, struggles with church changes and with religious life decisions. Always the inner question 'Why me?' accompanied any deep hurt or demands to let go. I kept asking, 'Why should I experience the hard things in life when I am trying my best to be good?' I also had an angry aching spirit. Over the years I developed an attitude that said life was always supposed to be a continuous hello. The hurt and wrenching ache of goodbye was not supposed to be there.

Eventually I accepted the fact that life is unfair at times, that it has its share of difficulties no matter how good I am or how much I am yearning for happiness. I began to realize that I could become a more whole human being because of the way that life sometimes pressed painfully against my happiness and my deep desire to have everything go well. I know that although I will sometimes feel broken apart or empty, eventually I will mend and be filled again.

Loss will never be easy for me, but I am much better at identifying the need to let go and at understanding the call to move on as a means of growth. Sometimes goodbyes still overwhelm me, but my questions are changing.

Instead of asking 'Why me?' I much more readily ask 'How?' – How can I move gracefully through the ache of the farewells that come into my life? I also ask 'Who?' – Who will be with me in this process? – because I know that I cannot go through intense leave-takings without some kinship and some loving support to sustain me.

These new questions have grown in my consciousness because of a very graced moment several years ago. The reality of my battle with goodbyes finally asserted itself one early morning as I walked across the beautiful University of Notre Dame campus. I found myself on a green lawn, facing a Pieta, a statuette of Mary, the Mother of Jesus, holding the body of her dead son. This particular statuette was shocking to me, stark and harsh, so unlike the soft, feminine touch of Michelangelo's *Woman and Son*. This Pieta had sharp, angular features. The figures were full of holes. It was a black, metallic affront to my eyes, speaking loudly of suffering, of pain and agony. I could hardly bear to look at it, and I wanted to run away. But something inside me drew me to sit and keep my eyes focused on the Woman of Sorrows who held her dead Son in her arms. Strong, powerful emotions pushed tears to my eyes. I hated the unfairness of life. I resented it in every fibre of my being. But I felt a deep yearning to discover a truth I had never possessed. As I looked and looked at the depiction of sorrow, the pain of goodbye seared through my gaze. I saw there a tremendous union of love, great strength, coupled with a heart-wrenching moment of lamentation and agony at life's unfairness. Truly this Pieta spoke more deeply the harsh truth of farewell than anything I had ever seen.

Deep within me the words came: 'You must face goodbyes. You must come to terms with life's unfairness. You cannot allow your "poor me's" and "not me's" to stunt your growth any longer. You need to use your energy to give life, not to fight death.' I continued to sit there for a long time.

When I arose, I knew what I had to do. I would walk the path of Jesus in a 30-day Ignatian retreat, a retreat that takes one right into the mystery of Holy Week and Easter with its loss and sorrow, its hope and resurrection. I would stop running. I'd throw myself into God's arms and I would ask God all those questions that were forever rising up to choke me. I would spend my days with Jesus: what would he say about life's losses? What was the meaning of his own life and suffering?

That moment of decision was one of the greatest graces of my life. My 30 days with God and a wonderful retreat directress changed my inner focus. So many essential, life-giving wisdoms surfaced during those days: the hello-goodbye pattern as an integral part of human existence, the necessity of change in order to have growth, and the need to let go before one can truly move on. I also learned that the cost of discipleship is inherent in any following of Jesus and that this following causes choices which mean goodbye to some parts of life and hello to others.

Most important, I discovered that for the Christian, hello always follows goodbye in some form if we allow it. There is, or can be, new life, although it will be different from the life we knew before. The resurrection of Jesus and the promises of God are too strong to have it be any other way.

1

The ache of autumn in us

There is a season for everything,
a time for giving birth,
a time for dying;
a time for tears,
a time for laughter;
a time for mourning,
a time for dancing. . .
    Ecclesiastes 3:1–2, 4

Autumn comes. It always does.
Goodbye comes. It always does.
The trees struggle with this truth today
and in my deepest of being, so do I.

Every autumn, nostalgia fills me;
every autumn, yearning holds me.
I cling to the ripeness of summer,
knowing it will be many long months
before I can catch a breath of lilac,
or the green of freshly mown grass.

And so I begin my fallow vigil,
remembering the truth of the ages:
Unless the wheat seed dies
it cannot sing a new birth.

Unless summer gives in to autumn
springtime will never embrace me.

Every autumn reminds me of my vulnerability. It carries the truth that life is fragile, that there are no sure guarantees for a trouble-free life, that there is always some dying in living, that change is inevitable. I was reminded of this in a particularly harsh way last October. There was a beautiful young linden tree just outside my office window. It was a golden glory in the sunshine, full of bright yellow, autumn leaves. One morning a strong wind came from the grey northeast sky. I stood and watched as every last leaf was stripped and torn away. In less than an hour the tree stood in nakedness, a golden circle of summer's growth at its feet.

I hurt for the tree in its emptiness. Then slowly I saw myself as the linden, moving through my own life stages, knowing how I, too, have sometimes felt the harsh blows of a ripping away. I stood by the window of my inner world and saw the story of transformation pass before me in invitation. At that moment I prayed hard and deep for openness and for the gift not to fight the process of good-bye.

But as I looked at the empty tree, my prayer became barely a whisper. All those beautiful leaves on the ground, the seemingly tragic stripping of a tree full of life! I felt that no part of me could easily say yes to an experience like that. As I turned away from the window I sensed a kinship with autumn. It had spoken loudly about the way life is with its going, grieving, growing story.

The ache of autumn that is in us has two faces. One is an ache that results from our own individual, particular losses – those farewells that are always going on in our lives.

The existential ache

One author speaks of an 'existential loneliness' that permeates every human spirit, a kind of unnamed pain inside, deep within us, a restlessness, an anxiety, a sense of 'all aloneness' that calls out to us. I prefer to name it an 'existential ache'. It is a persistent longing in us and it happens because we are human. It is as strongly present in us as autumn is present in the cycle of the seasons. I believe that this ache is within us because we are composed of both physical and spiritual dimensions. Our body belongs to the earth but our spirit does not. Our final home is not here, although 'here' is where we are meant to be transformed by treasuring, reverencing and growing through our human journey. No matter how good the 'good earth' is, there is always a part of us that is yearning, longing, quietly crying out for the true homeland where life is no longer difficult or unfair.

Every once in a while we get in touch with this truth in us. It is not a sadness exactly, not a hurt or a pain as such, but some tremendously deep voice that cries out in bitter-sweet agony. We catch a glimpse of how far we have yet to go; we see that there are many twists and bends and struggles in the road before we arrive home, and this glimpse pains us with its reality. It is the autumn in all of us, the truth that life can never stay just as it is.

This inner ache is felt especially when we sense the mystery of life or the supreme uniqueness of who we are. It is present when we recognize the fleetingness of all that we know and all that we cling to upon this good earth. We have a strong longing at this moment to hold onto all of it and we realize the impossibility of doing so. We seldom put words to this melancholy. We only dimly sense its presence. But it colours our moods and pervades our activities and weaves its way through our unconscious.

It is present in our edginess or in blue days that seem to have no cause. It raises its voice in our inability to concentrate or to feel full satisfaction, even when everything in our lives is going smoothly. It makes itself felt when, perhaps just for a brief moment, we recognize our mortality and the swiftness with which time passes.

There will always be a corner of our heart where it is autumn, that part of us which aches with searching and loneliness, with restlessness or dissatisfaction. It is Augustine's 'Our hearts are made for you, O Lord, and they will not rest until they rest in you'. It will remain in us until we are truly home.

What about those who never seem to have this experience? Some never recognize the ache for what it is, while others push away these feelings and awarenesses as far from themselves as possible. They cannot bear the message. The ache is not comfortable and some ignore it or run away from it by being so busy that they do not have time to think or feel anything too deeply. Some press harder in their work; some rush out to buy things when they feel lonely or down. Some always seek out others so they will not have to listen to that sense of incompleteness within themselves. Radios and televisions that are always on may be attempts to block out the truth that lies within.

Not that we should be self-absorbed by our inner ache, but it is very worthwhile to acknowledge it. This loneliness, paradoxically, joins us with all others in their aloneness. There is a great strength and comfort in this. It is only when we are willing to meet the absolute truth of that aloneness within us that we are no longer alone, that we are able to break through to a level of consciousness that assures us of the magnificent bonding that we have with other humans and with God. We begin to see the ache as a natural part of our humanity and of our inner journey. This awareness and bonding can be a source of a deep and rich spiritual growth. We realize that we are not the only ones who are going home, we are not the only ones whose lives call us to many partings before we are at one with the eternal hello. Kenneth Leech expresses it this way:

> True self-love means not trying to escape from ourselves, but listening to the voices within us. . . . This involves the acceptance of our fundamental aloneness, not seeking to reduce it, not hoping that friendship, marriage, community, or group, will take it away. That aloneness is an integral part of being human, and an essential element in love. It is out of that aloneness that it becomes possible to respond rather than merely react to people and needs. Response has to grow and emerge out of the depths of myself: it is *my* response, born out of my inner struggle and inner self-knowledge, out of my spirit, my deepest core. This is what spirituality is about.[1]

If we are attentive to the inner ache, and if we grow in accepting its truthful message, then we will more readily move through our own particular goodbyes. We will be more open to the growth of the human journey.

The ache of particular goodbyes

Goodbyes are a part of every single day. Sometimes we choose them, and sometimes they choose us. Usually they are small, the not so significant losses that do not pain us very much, but at times they are deep, powerful, wounding experiences that trail around our hearts and cause pain inside us for years.

What is a goodbye? It is an empty place in us. It is any situation in which there is some kind of loss, some incompleteness, when a space is created in us that cries out to be filled. Goodbyes are any of those times when we find ourselves without a someone or a something that has given our life meaning and value, when a dimension of our life seems to be out of place or unfulfilled. Goodbyes are all of those experiences that leave us with a hollow feeling somewhere deep inside.

We say goodbye to parents, spouses, children, friends, sometimes just for a day or a year, and sometimes until we meet them on the other side of this life. We leave familiar places and secure homes. We bid farewell to strong, healthy bodies, burden-free spirits or minds. We change teachers, schools, parishes and managers, sometimes spouses or religion. We change our ideas, our values, our self-image and our way of interpreting life's situations. We place parents in nursing homes, allow children to experience risk-taking and growth, say no to love relationships that would be inappropriate or possibly harmful to us or to others. All these hard decisions and choices that we make or experience involve some kind of leave-taking.

In our work world we experience transfers, changes in skills, different positions and retirement; in natural disasters such as fires, floods, storms of all kinds, we lose significant material possessions that can never be reclaimed. Illness, whether our own or of loved ones, demands a farewell to some of our independence or to our mobility and strength, to our energy and, perhaps, to our sexual drive. We say goodbye through our ageing process. We bid adieu to a part of ourselves and others as children grow up and grow away, as we experience relationship adjustments on all levels. There are goodbyes in our ongoing conversion of heart when we let go of non-truths, of sinful, worn ways or old angers or antipathies that have consumed us. We also experience farewells in adult transitions where we struggle with self-image, goals and dreams. It may be a time of letting go of our hope of being the best, or of having the perfect parents or the perfect family or the perfect community. These goodbyes that seem to last forever reflect the inner ache of autumn with its hollowness and emptiness.

Identifying our goodbyes

When the goodbyes are big ones such as the death of a loved one or a divorce, we have no trouble recognizing them. It is the lesser goodbyes that we can avoid or not acknowledge and, in doing so, miss the inner direction and the value of growth they offer us. The following questions may be of help in identifying those goodbyes.

1 *What hurts you now?*
   What distresses you, worries you, causes you negative feelings, such as anger, envy, jealousy, self-pity, discouragement, anxiety, fear? Is there any part of your life that feels lost?

2 *What do you wish you could get rid of in your life?*
   Is it a deep sense of loss due to the death of a loved one, your own illness or a physical pain, a problem at work or at home, a great loneliness, a sinfulness, the hurried pace of life, some guilt, irritating persons, your own lack of mental or spiritual or social growth, another's illness, your own ageing, an old memory, an enemy? What would you like to never have to experience again?

3 *What do you wish that you could have more of in your life?*
   Would it be faith, friendships, personal giftedness and talents, money, hope, sense of direction, security, good

health, a feeling of being that special someone in another's life, time to be with those you love, companionship, freedom, truth? What is it that you most yearn for?

4 *How does it hurt you?*

Is your response one of self-preoccupation or self-centredness, bodily distress, poor self-image or lack of belief in self, depression, distrust, keeping others shut out, anxiety attacks, misdirected anger, loneliness, emptiness, loss of security, lack of concentration, feelings of failure? How are you (or how is your life) different because of this hurt?

Once we recognize and come to terms with how a goodbye is hurting us, we can begin the process of working with it. For example, if we are letting our pain take us too far from others and too much into self-centredness, we can begin taking steps to get more involved in the lives of others. If our goodbye is affecting our lack of peace by its anger or bitterness, we can begin to acknowledge those feelings, expressing them in a healthy way and gradually be freed of them. Only after we have acknowledged our losses and have recognized the pain inherent in these goodbyes can we proceed on the journey of self-growth and greater love of others.

The value of goodbyes

Goodbyes, especially the more intense ones, cause us to face the ultimate questions of life: Why suffering? Where am I heading? What are my most cherished values? What do I believe about life after death? Goodbyes create a certain space in us where we allow ourselves room to look at life in perspective and to gradually discover answers to some of those questions about life. We also learn a lot about the significant others in our lives: we learn who is willing to walk the long road with us, whose heart always welcomes us no matter what, who loves us enough to stand with us in good times and in bad, who is willing to love us enough to speak the truth for us or to us. Goodbyes, when reflected upon in faith, can draw us to a greater reliance upon the God of love, our most significant other. With God we can learn to live in hope, with greater meaning and deeper joy. All this only comes with time and with great care of self.

We all need to learn how to say goodbye, to acknowledge the pain that is there for us so that we can eventually move on to another hello. When we learn how to say goodbye we truly learn how to say to ourselves and to others: 'Go, God be with you. I entrust you to God. The God of strength, courage, comfort, hope, love, is with you. The God who promises to wipe away all tears will hold you close and will fill your emptiness. Let go and be free to move on. Do not keep yourself from another step in your homeward journey. May the blessing of the God of autumn be with you.'

Questions for reflection, integration, discussion

1 Write down the word *autumn*. Next to it (or under it) jot down words and phrases that come to your mind as you think of this season. What is your predominant feeling about autumn?

2 What are the goodbyes that are currently happening in your life? Which is the hardest for you? What makes it so difficult?

3 What is the goodbye through which you have experienced the most growth? What made it so creative for you?

2

I know how the flowers felt

The rain to the wind said,
'You push and I'll pelt.'
They so smote the garden bed
That the flowers actually knelt,
And lay lodged – though not dead.
I know how the flowers felt.[1]

Robert Frost

If you have ever said a deeply significant goodbye, you know 'how the flowers felt'. You know what it is like to have life pelt you with sorrow, to be overwhelmed with emptiness, loneliness, confusion and sadness. At these times we are bent over, crushed, like the flowers that 'lay lodged – though not dead'. The pain is overwhelming, often too deep for tears. The sorrow of it can pervade one's whole self and hurt in every part of one's being. No medicine, no bandage, no diversion, no luxury, no words can assuage the hurt and give it the freedom to desist and cease its painful bending, almost breaking, of the heart. Time and the strength of God's presence can lessen the pain, but even these gifts cannot take the pain away or cure it completely. Just when we think that the last bit of goodbye is out of our heart, we hear someone's name, or we recall a memory, or we have another dream, or an old wound of the spirit flares up in our consciousness, and the pain is suddenly very real again.

Every goodbye has some suffering in it and the greater the parting the deeper the pain; the greater the loss, the more severe is the empty place that accompanies it. Some of us feel the hurt more than others. So much depends on our personality, our personal history, our relationship with God, and our own philosophy of life. People who are deep-feeling will usually ache over goodbyes a great deal more than those who approach life on a more intellectual, analytical level. People whose families brush the hurt of loss aside or cover it up with silence, busyness or other ways of avoidance will probably find themselves doing the same thing, not realizing how intense the loss actually is. No matter how we stuff it away or avoid it, however, the pain of goodbyes will show itself in our lives at some time.

I listen to the story of one who has lost a dearly beloved spouse and I wonder if there can be any goodbye so deep as that death in a person's life. I hear the agony of one who has recently been divorced, who has experienced the death of love itself. 'Surely,' I say to myself, 'this goodbye is one of the deepest wounds of all.' Then a young man comes into my life, talented and promising, and he suffers a broken neck in a swimming accident, paralysed for life, forced to say goodbye to many of his dreams for the future. I realize how intense his inner pain is. I meet a man who has been in deep depression because of a forced early retirement. He tells me with tears in his eyes how his whole identity has been that of his work world. He has spent a year struggling with questions about the value of his life and its purpose. It has been a year full of suffering.

The stories go on and on and so does the hurt inherent in them. No two people say goodbye in exactly the same way and no two people suffer their farewells in the same way, but suffer they do. That is why the mystery of suffering must be considered when one is reflecting on the losses in life.

The painful feelings that accompany any grieving process or time of loss are on all levels of our being: physical, emotional, mental and spiritual. When we grieve, we leave behind someone or something very precious to us. We can expect to have any or all of the following feelings: shock, sadness, depression, denial. There may be volatile emotions of hostility or intense yearnings, tearfulness, restlessness, fears and anxieties of all kinds. We may feel that there is no one who can understand our grief. We may not be able to concentrate on our work or our responsibilities and we may even think that we are losing our minds because we feel so disoriented and fragmented inside. We will probably be angry and feel guilty over something unsaid or undone. We might have resentment and self-pity for a time. There is often a sense of being lost. We may feel that no one cares, not even God who has always been there for us. There may also be pain in our body where there was never pain before: headaches, backaches, stomach aches or other symptoms. During our darkest and loneliest of times, we are sometimes frightened by our loss of enthusiasm, our thoughts of 'Why go on?' or of 'Why even bother to get out of bed today?' We often feel drained of the desire to do anything that requires our investment and our energy. It is hard to go on believing and trying to live during times of great loss.[2]

The suffering and the sensation of hurting deep within our personal system gradually diminishes with time. At the moment we are experiencing the anguish of the goodbye, however, it seems as though it will never go away. We feel like the flowers, crushed and overwhelmed by the inner storm.

These painful feelings come in varying degrees with the many forms of goodbye that are a part of life. They also come when we deliberately make certain choices. We say farewell to other options when we accept the decisions we have made. Suffering is especially sharp when the choices are between options that both look beneficial: Do I go on that trip with my spouse who so much needs my presence now in his mid-life struggle, or do I stay at home with our children who are at such a crucial adolescent age? Do I continue with chemotherapy which makes me so ill but prolongs my life, or do I discontinue it and enjoy the quality of life I now have? Do I place my mother in a nursing home where health care is so much better, or do I continue to support her in the situation of living alone where she feels so much more secure and at peace but is also much more prone to accidents? Do I file for divorce because it is so obvious that my marriage has died and is death-dealing to both my spouse and to myself, or do I go on choosing to remain in the situation because the children need the two of us to be there for them? Often it is very hard to live peacefully with the choices that one has to make.

Life is unfair

Much of how we learn to live and grow through the suffering of our goodbyes has to do with how we look at the cause of that suffering. When people are in the middle of hard moments, when they are trying to account for 'life accidents' (those unplanned for, unpredictable parts of life), they often try to find someone or something to explain their cause.[3] People who are suffering often conclude that life is unfair. But what they may actually mean is: Why isn't God fair? The expectation is that good should come to the good and bad to the bad. If we have been good we should not have the hard, ugly blows of life.

Isn't that how God ought to operate? Why isn't God fair? Isn't God the one who is ultimately to blame for this pain? Couldn't this God, who can do all things, have stopped it in an instant?

How often this attitude towards suffering is voiced by those who have been hurt because of goodbyes. Parents who have taken so much time with their children and have done their best to share good values with them are wounded by their children's choices of lifestyles and substance abuse: drug taking, glue sniffing and so on. Their inner voices are a mixture of guilt and anger at life's unfairness: Where did we go wrong? Why has life dealt us this humiliating blow? Why has God let this happen? The woman who battles against depression all her life wonders the same thing. Something in her keeps pulling at her self-esteem and dragging away her joy as she goes on saying goodbye to her inner energy and enthusiasm. She looks at others who have never had this long, emotional war and she wonders: Why me? What have I done? What more could I do? Why hasn't God taken this away? A man who deeply loves his wife and struggles hard to make life good for her and their five children is left in loneliness after her death in a car accident. He cries out in anger and agony: Why my wife? Why me? Why us? Why didn't you prevent the accident, God? Or the woman who wakes up one day to discover that the husband she has felt so close to has chosen a new life with one of his employees. She is wracked with the pain of betrayal and personal rejection and she, too, cries out that she has been given something that she doesn't deserve. The farmer who has worked and worked to hold on to his land is given the devastating decision of foreclosure by his bank. Market prices, drought and storms were too much for him. He walks across his land for one last time saying goodbye to a way of life that has meant so much, and he wonders what he did wrong that life could treat him so cruelly. All of these people have come face to face with a reality of the human condition: life *is* unfair. Life does not always treat us kindly. They have also come face to face with the deep questions of goodbyes: What does God have to do with my suffering? Why does life have to be this way?

False theories about suffering

A woman recently shared with me how she had tried to account for the pain in her life. She had suffered from osteoporosis for a major portion of her life and was always hurting, in and out of the hospital with broken bones. One evening she had an opportunity to go to a healing service. She said to the minister, 'I don't know what I'm doing here; I think God wants me to have this suffering for a reason.' The minister replied, 'God doesn't want you to have this. God wants you to be whole, happy in body, mind and spirit.' She looked at him in surprise and said, 'Well, if God didn't send this to me, who *can* I blame?'

Who can we blame? If we listen closely to those who hurt or those who are trying to console someone who hurts, we can hear in their remarks a certain belief about who causes suffering and why. Their beliefs usually centre around one of the following reasons. First, God sends the hurt, the bitter loss, because he loves us so much. Thus, the greater our difficulties, the greater is God's love for us because suffering is a purification and a means of transformation. Another belief says that God sends pain because we are being punished for some sin of the past. There is guilt in this belief and often added sorrow because of the sufferer's feelings that, indirectly, they caused God to send the suffering. They believe the suffering would not have happened had it not been for their sin. (Like the young couple who were deeply grieved at the death of their two-year-old son. When he died they concluded that God had taken their child because he was born out of wedlock.) Thirdly, some think that God sends the suffering to test them, to see if they really have faith and to prove their love for God in times of trial. Finally, there is a belief that God sends suffering for some reason that we do not understand. People often say, 'It is God's will for us and we must simply accept it if we are to be good and faithful followers.'

Not one of these four beliefs is an accurate approach for understanding the suffering of our broken places or for living through them. The major premise in all of these beliefs is false. *God does not send suffering to us.* We still have a lot of unhealthy thinking in our theology of suffering. Whenever we say 'God sends suffering' we are entering into pagan-tinged territory. In ancient times people also struggled with the ache and pain that came into their human existence. They questioned the elements — Why lightning and storms that destroyed? Why infertility for some women and not for others? Why death, disease or other calamities that crippled and stole life? They began to see all these mysterious struggles as coming from some hidden power in the situation. Something or someone was sending them good or bad things. They developed a theory that if they appeased the mysterious powers, which they presumed caused good or bad to happen, then they would be spared life's travails and pains. The gods, as these powers were later named, would then be good to them in return and would not send them suffering.

This theology of suffering, based on an appeasement of the gods who had power over them, was carried over into Old Testament stories. Recall the story of Abraham who was asked to kill his only son on the altar of sacrifice to prove his faith in the true God (Gn 22). A messenger of

God entered in and stopped Abraham. When this happened a tradition of thought was broken: no more human sacrifices to appease the one true God. It was a breakthrough, but the idea of sacrifices of appeasement persisted for a long, long time as we can see in the New Testament approach that refers to Jesus as being a scapegoat or an appeasement sacrifice to the Father (1 Cor 6:20; 1 Pet 1:19; Heb 10:1–18).

The testing approach to suffering has also been held for many years. In the story of Job the author tells us that God tested Job by destroying everyone that Job loved and everything of value that Job owned. What kind of God would do this? The author of the Book of Job was struggling with the mystery of suffering just as we do and concluded that God was a testing God.

The thought that God sends suffering as a punishment for our sins is expressed throughout humanity's history, throughout the Old Testament and in the New Testament. When Jesus is with the disciples they ask him about a blind man: 'Rabbi, who sinned, this man or his parents, for him to have been born blind?' Jesus answered them, 'Neither he nor his parents sinned. He was born blind so that the works of God might be displayed in him' (Jn 9:2–3). At another time Jesus himself raised the same kind of question in order to dispel the theory of suffering as a punishment for sin. When 'some people arrived and told him about the Galileans whose blood Pilate had mingled with that of their sacrifices', Jesus said to them, 'Do you suppose these Galileans who suffered like that were greater sinners than any other Galileans? They were not, I tell you' (Lk 13:1–3). In both cases Jesus is refuting the long-held belief that the suffering of the man born blind, or of the murdered Galileans or of anyone in a similar position, is a punishment for sin. In each of these circumstances, Jesus goes on to point out the necessity of repenting of one's sinfulness and suggests that instances such as these can be invitations for a change of heart or for inner conversion. In doing this, he implies that suffering *can* be an opportunity for us to reflect on our life, the kind of persons we are, how we relate to others, what we value, but Jesus flatly refuses to uphold the traditional theory that suffering is sent as a punishment for one's sins.

What about the will of God? Does God will our suffering? No, God does not send our suffering or want us to have it, but God does allow it to be there. Jesus himself struggled with the 'will of the Father' when he was in his moment of agony (Lk 22:39–46). Jesus was fully human. He did not want the pain. He begged his Father to enter into his goodbye moment and to take away the pain: 'Father,' he said, 'if you are willing, take this cup away from me.' When Jesus continued with, 'Nevertheless, let your will be done, not mine,' he was accepting his painful situation. The Father did not enter in, did not perform a miracle and keep him from the cross; he did not save Jesus from being human. He allowed Jesus to have full participation in the human condition just as all of us have to enter fully into it. God's will for us is that of our happiness, our peace of mind and heart. God does not will us or want us to suffer life's hurts, but God does allow the suffering to happen because, as Rabbi Kushner says so clearly, for God to do otherwise would be to block our human nature and our human condition.[4] Accidents do happen, death does come to us all, disease is prevalent in our world, but God is not *doing* these things to us. We are full and finite human beings living on an earth where natural disasters occur, where genetic conditions exist, where we sometimes make poor or sinful choices, where life does not always work out as we had planned and hoped it would. We are blessed and burdened with our humanity, with the mystery of growing into a wholeness of personhood which involves continual goodbyes. We are frail and unfinished, subject always to the possibility of pain. We live in a world where we know we cannot escape our own mortality, our final goodbye before the eternal hello.

A God who cares

When we experience our goodbyes, we come face to face with questions about suffering. We also come face to face with a God who suffers pain and hurts with us, a God who wants us to be free of our suffering. Jesus gave evidence of this in his life by blessing and healing, freeing and consoling, doing all he could to take away the suffering that was part of the human condition. God is one who has promised over and over in the Scriptures to be near with comfort for us, to be there to sustain us, to keep us from being destroyed by our difficulties (2 Cor 4:7–18; Rom 8:35–39; Is 43:1–5). This God is a refuge for the needy in distress, a shelter from the storm, a shade from the heat (Is 25:4), the good friend who stays with us in our struggles and our emptiness. I think of this God as being revealed in the woman in my community who comforted me when I received the phone call telling of my young brother's death. She came up and put her arm around my shoulders and held me as I cried. What a wonderful comfort I felt at that moment. I was not alone in my pain; I knew she cared; I knew she was there feeling the pain with me.

This God who stays with us in our struggles is the one described to me in a letter from a friend. She wrote:

There is some resistance in me when dealing with my own pain and grief and relating it to God. I have had two experiences of God being with me in my suffering of the past three years. Part of me knew of

God's care, love and concern for me through the care, love and concern of those around me. It was in that that I began discovering the responsibility I carried for my own life – and that God wasn't going to change events for me but would help me grow through them.

This compassionate, caring God is 'like a shepherd feeding his flock, gathering the lambs in his arms, holding them against his breast' (Is 40:11). Isaiah tells us that we are so close to God that we are carved on the palm of God's hand, and that we will never be forgotten by him (Is 49:14–16). This is the God who consoles us when we feel our brokenness:

'Do not be afraid, for I have redeemed you;
I have called you by your name, you are mine.
Should you pass through the sea, I will be there with you;
or through rivers, they will not swallow you up.
Should you walk through fire, you will not be scorched and the flames will not burn you. . . .
You are precious in my eyes. . . I love you. . . .
Do not be afraid, for I am with you' (Is 43:2, 4).

God's love is such a powerful companion for us that no matter how searing or how intense the hurt of a loss is we know that our spirit need not be destroyed by it; we know that God will help us to recover our hope, our courage and our direction in life.

If we allow ourselves to know God in this way, then we will have a very different approach to the will of God. As the authors of *Compassion* tell us:

God's will is not a label that can be put on unhappy

situations. . . . Instead of declaring anything and everything to be the will of God, we must be willing to ask ourselves where in the midst of our pains and sufferings we can discern this loving presence of God.[5]

This loving presence of God can be our stronghold in our goodbyes. Our image of God is so important when we come to terms with suffering. If God is a God 'out there' who is always demanding hard things for us in order to purify us or punish us, or if God is seen as always sending us sorrows in order to test us or challenge us to do some divine 'will', or if God is seen as piling on suffering in order to show how much we are loved, then we will draw little comfort and consolation from our relationship with God during our goodbye times. We may, in fact, feel a lot of anger, bitterness, guilt and resentment towards this God.

Our awareness of the loving presence of God does not mean that we will never have moments of feeling angry at God or abandoned by God or be just plain unfeeling towards God during times of loss. These are natural, human responses of grief and some feel them more strongly than others. But we will not go on forever blaming God for causing the situation or for not intervening and stopping the event. If our image of God is a positive one, we will eventually return to a time when we recognize the comfort and love that are waiting there for us.

Our God is a God who dwells within, a loving presence near to us who yearns for our happiness, one who walks with us in our struggles. If our God is a God who holds us close 'as a mother hen gathers her chicks' close to her (Mt 23:37), then we will come through our goodbyes with a deeper sense of being tenderly cared for by our God and we will draw comfort and strength from this presence. As

Kushner writes:

> We can't pray that God will make our lives free of
> problems; this won't happen, and it is probably just
> as well. ... But people who pray for courage, for
> strength to bear the unbearable, for the grace to
> remember what they have left instead of what they
> have lost, very often find their prayers answered.
> They discover that they have more strength, more
> courage than they ever knew themselves to have.
> Where did they get it? I would like to think that their
> prayers helped them find that strength. Their
> prayers helped them to tap reserves of faith and
> courage which were not available to them before.[6]

Our one-liners

Besides our understanding of the relationship
between God and life's unfairness, there is another
very vital element in our ability to grow through a
goodbye moment. I call this element our 'one-liners',
those sayings we have inside us which sum up our
vision or philosophy of life.

Our one-liners tell us a lot about what gets us
through the tough times. Some that people have
shared with me are:

This, too, will pass.

One day at a time.

In the end, it will all be OK.

Expect the unexpected.

No pain – no gain.

Make the most of each day.

Be good to yourself.

Life is a gift, never to be taken for granted.

Everyone needs to have another chance.

Even a perfect egg must break for new life to begin.

Life is what we make it.

Sometimes these one-liners wear thin or no longer have the power they once had for us and we need to find new ones because we have changed and we have grown.

Nietzsche said, 'The one who has a *why* to live can bear with almost any *how*.' Our philosophy of life often comes from wise persons we have known personally or through history. Viktor Frankl's vision of life has most influenced my own one-liners and has greatly enabled me to see that suffering can be a means of growth in wisdom and strength. Frankl was a psychotherapist who experienced the concentration camps. He was prisoner No 119,104 at Auschwitz. There Frankl was stripped naked in his existence; everyone and everything he cherished was taken from him. In spite of his intense aloneness and loneliness, in spite of the horror of non-human conditions, Viktor Frankl not only survived the camp but developed a deep understanding of the human spirit. He searched to find meaning in life through his sufferings and he believed that if there were a purpose in life at all, there must be a purpose in suffering and dying. He firmly believed that our attitude towards suffering makes all the difference in how we live our lives. In *Man's Search for Meaning* he says:

When a man finds that it is his destiny to suffer, he

will have to accept that suffering as his task; the single unique task. He will have to acknowledge the fact that even in suffering he is unique and alone in the universe. No one can relieve him of the suffering or suffer in his place. His unique opportunity lies in the way in which he bears his burden.[7]

The way that Viktor Frankl bore his burdens helped him to grow through the many goodbyes to loved ones, and to human dignity and freedom during his time at Auschwitz. The way that we bear our burdens can do the same. We have a choice in our theology of suffering and we have a choice in our response to the suffering that comes our way. We can respond with anger and bitterness by being stoical and not allowing ourselves to cry or to have anyone comfort us. We can be the martyr, full of self-pity, bemoaning our pain forever and becoming self-centred. We can give up, let ourselves stay depressed, stop trying to put life into our life, or we can gradually grow wiser and find deeper meaning in our existence.

We will probably experience many negative responses and feelings in our grieving (it is natural to do so), but if our vision of life is whole and hopeful, our goodbye pain will eventually lead us to compassion and to a deeper bonding with others who know hurt and sorrow. We will find ourselves readily and warmly embracing others who grieve because we have been down that long, lonely road of goodbyes and we know how blessed it is to have the touch of care beside us. We will not only know 'how the flowers felt', we will also know the powerful strength of a God who goes with us on that goodbye journey when we are bent over from the storms of life. It is this loving God who will enable our empty places to become sources of transformation, inner wisdom, compassion and tenderness.

Questions for reflection, integration, discussion:

1 How do *you* explain life's unfairness?
2 We have wise persons in our lives who have given us insights into suffering. Who is your wise person and what have you learned from him or her?
3 What is the one-liner that gets you through the suffering in your life?
4 What is your vision or philosophy of life? These questions will help you to put words on it:

Who/what is most important to you in your life?

What is most helpful for your personal growth?

How do you feel about change?

How do you usually respond to life's accidents?

What significance does God or religious faith have for you?

If you had only one year to live, how would you want to spend this time?

What do you want people to remember about you after you die?

3

Hello – Goodbye – Hello

A woman in childbirth suffers
because her time has come;
but when she has given birth to
   the child she forgets the
   suffering
in her joy that (a child) has been
   born into the world.
So it is with you: you are sad now,
but I shall see you again, and your
   hearts will be full of joy,
and that joy no one shall take from you.
   John 16:21–22

What does the life and message of Jesus tell us about the
goodbyes in our lives? It tells us that he knew what it was
like to go through those painful times. He, too, had many
moments when he felt pulled apart, knew the hurt of
leaving behind, felt the emptiness that comes with deep
loss. Jesus was not spared the ache and the struggle of
letting go. He knew the price of goodbyes. They had been
with him all his life because he was so fully human, so
much like all of us who travel the hello-goodbye-hello
pattern of the human journey.

We do not know much about the years before his move
out of Nazareth. We do know that 'he grew in wisdom and

stature . . .' (Lk 2:52). Because he was like us in all things except sin (Heb 4:15), we can only presume that he went through many of the goodbyes that other people his age experienced: growing pains of adolescence and self-identity, sorrowing over relatives who died, developing friendships and struggling with them, seeing his parents age, improving his work skills while sometimes failing at what he tried. Beyond these presumptions about his early years, we do know that leave-taking was a familiar part of the last three years of his life. It began with a goodbye to almost 30 years of security in his hometown, where a tug inside him said, 'It's time you moved on'. It was time for him to walk away from everyone and everything that he had known – his home, his family, his friends, his work, his favourite places of recreation, relaxation and prayer, his at-homeness with the town and the surrounding area.

The walk away from his secure world took Jesus into a very significant rite of passage: his 40 days in the desert where he said a prayerful farewell to all those years of Nazareth and came to terms with the letting go that was being asked of him. He felt a power within himself that pulled him forth into a whole new world of ministry. Luke tells us that Jesus left the desert 'with the power of the Spirit in him' (Lk 4:14). It was the power to say goodbye in order to say hello.

It was this power working in him and the ever-deepening love of his Father that enabled Jesus to walk into the mobility and insecurity of his ministry. He who had always had a place to lay his head for almost 30 years suddenly had no home, only a constant movement from one place to another (Lk 9:58). Life became one continual journey of deep investment and letting go, of rooting and uprooting, of settling down and of moving on. Even though Jesus was constantly on the go, however, he allowed himself to develop friendships, to love deeply, knowing it would mean the price of farewell. Some of the people with whom he invested his time and love were Mary, Martha and their brother Lazarus. They were good friends whose home in Bethany was a shelter and a comfort to him (Jn 11:1–2; 12:1–8; Lk 10:38–42). How renewed and rested he must have been after he had stopped there on his travels. Yet, Jesus knew he would have to get up and leave again after his visits. He could never just stay comfortable and secure in the place where he felt so at home, where he felt loved, respected, understood and accepted.

As Jesus got up and moved on, he met many who were experiencing loss in their lives: parents whose children had died, men and women who had known great emotional or physical pain, all kinds of people with all sorts of goodbyes wrapped around their hearts. Jesus showed compassion and he grieved with them. He often stopped along the way to comfort people in their hurts. He ached over their sufferings. 'He took pity on them and healed their sick' (Mt 14:14). Jesus reached out and led them to hellos of good health, new vision of body or of spirit, to mental or emotional well-being, and to renewed inner life.

As he comforted others, Jesus continued to have his own farewells. His friend Mary tearfully told him of her brother's death, the brother whom Jesus greatly loved. The Scriptures tell us that Jesus was so distressed that his sigh 'came straight from the heart' and that he wept as he stood there before the tomb. So great was his sadness that those who stood nearby said, 'See how much he loved him!' (Jn 11:36).

Jesus wept again in a very different situation. He was coming to Jerusalem, returning from a journey, possibly reflecting on his trip, on his hopes and longings for the people of his ministry. The yearning in his heart was so great that 'as he drew near and came in sight of the city he shed tears over it and said, "If you in your turn had only understood on this day the message of peace!"' (Lk 19:41–42). He lamented and was pained over all that he wanted for the people: 'How often have I longed to gather your children, as a hen gathers her chicks under her wings, and you refused!' (Mt 23:37–38). It was a painful moment for Jesus as he dealt with yet another goodbye: he could not force the people to wake up to the truth of the kingdom. He had to let go of being able to do that. When I have heard parents weeping over children who have gone astray, when I have listened to the pain of church ministers who dreamed so much for a congregation that was immersed in its own selfish ambitions, when I have been with anyone who cried because the goodness they so intensely wanted to share had been rejected, I have thought of Jesus weeping over a people that refused to listen to his love and to change their ways.

Scripture does not tell us that Jesus wept over his cousin John's beheading, but it does imply that he needed time to grieve over the death of this good man for whom he had such high regard, the one of whom he said, 'Of all children born of women, a greater than John the Baptist has never been seen' (Mt 11:11). When Jesus received the news of John's death, 'he withdrew by boat to a lonely place where they could be by themselves' (Mt 14:13). Tears of goodbye must have hung in the heart of Jesus as he grieved the going of his dear cousin.

There were all those other moments, too, when he had to let the grief stir inside, and just live with it and accept it. He said goodbye to the respect of those in leadership and authority, to being understood by his disciples, and to being accepted in his own town when he went home. It was people of his own hometown who 'sprang to their feet and hustled him out of town . . . intending to throw him down the cliff' (Lk 4:16–30). Yes, Jesus has been there before us in the hurt of rejection, non-acceptance and lack of understanding.

'The emptied one'

All of these powerful events were part of the goodbye experience in the life of Jesus. Just as each of us has many daily losses throughout our life, so, too, with Jesus. And just as each of us has the large, significant, jolting, sometimes devastating goodbyes, so, too, with Jesus. It was the passion and death of Jesus which was the culmination and totality of his goodbyes, where his body and spirit were surrendered to the pain of leave-taking. He 'emptied himself', letting go of all security and defences, fully vulnerable to the pain of the human condition which was his (Phil 2:6–11).

As we reflect on this emptiness of Jesus, let us look at the Last Supper. This scene is a goodbye holding many goodbyes. It was a farewell meal and speech to his friends; it was the terrible recognition that one of those dear to him was actually going to betray him, and that one of them would deny that he ever knew him. It was also the pain of coming nearer to his own death and it was a time when he could look back over his years of ministry, saying goodbye to all that he had not yet accomplished, remembering those he wept over as he approached Jerusalem.

All of these goodbyes were present but there was a unique and penetrating pain that took hold of Jesus that evening. It was an agonizing tension. On the one hand, he yearned to be with the 'Abba' whose magnificent bonding claimed his heart, and on the other, he desired to be with those he loved so dearly through his life and ministry. Jesus knew the sadness and the ache in their hearts;

he felt it keenly, and it only intensified his struggle with his own goodbyes. 'One day when they were together in Galilee, Jesus said to them, "The Son of Man is going to be handed over into the power of men; they will put him to death, and on the third day he will be raised to life again." And a great sadness came over them' (Mt 17:22–23). The intense desire to be with his Father did not lessen the love which Jesus had for his friends. It only increased the ache within him as he felt the strain of departure coming upon him.

It was the powerful bond which Jesus had with his Abba that sustained him as he experienced the struggle of farewell. If Jesus had a one-liner that carried him through the emptiness of his goodbyes it was almost certainly: *I am going to the Father* (Jn 14:12). Jesus's relationship with his Father was one that grew and deepened and matured. He had come to know that he was truly the Beloved Son (Lk 3:22) and this vision centred in his heart, took a powerful hold in him, a truth that seared his depths with love. By the time that Jesus had reached that intense farewell of the last meal with his disciples, his yearning to be with his Father was a poignant, painful drawing in his heart. What tension was in him, wanting so much to complete that journey, yet struggling with paying the price of goodbye to get there.

Chapters 13 to 17 of John's gospel are filled with fragments of goodbye messages, beautiful speeches by Jesus where he attempts to have his disciples understand that he is leaving them, that the time has come for him to depart. They are the final goodbye messages of a dying one to the beloved. He expresses his love for them over and over again and tells them to not be afraid and troubled, but to be brave and to trust in the Father, to believe that they will one day be with him. Jesus calls them his dear friends and makes one final request that they carry on his work by loving one another. Time and again Jesus refers to the underlying strength in himself; 'I am going to the Father' (Jn 14:28). 'I am going to the one who sent me' (Jn 16:5). 'As the Father has loved me . . .' (Jn 15:9). 'The Father is with me' (Jn 16:32). Finally, he pours out his heart to his Father. Chapter 17 is a magnificent prayer of one who is coming to terms with having to pray the price of goodbye. He knows his hour has come as he reflects on his life. He stands before the Father, ready to give all, deeply desiring to go home:

'I came from the Father and have come into the world and now I leave the world to go to the Father.'

(Jn 16:28)

'Father, the hour has come . . .
I am coming to you.'

(Jn 17:1, 11)

'But now I am coming to you
and while still in the world I say these things
to share my joy with them to the full.'   (Jn 17:13)

Once Jesus had said his farewells and had braved the sadness of his last meal before his death, he went forth to walk the road of total abandonment. He knew he needed strength to endure the deep emptiness which awaited him. He needed time with his Father at one of his favourite prayer places. He asked his close friends to stand by him as he struggled with the pain. It was here in the olive garden that Jesus faced his fear of what lay ahead, begging the Father to spare him if he would, but always open to what would be. How much added intensity of pain it was for Jesus when his friends did not watch with him, did not stand by him as he agonized over the future. He loved them so totally and they would not be present to him when he most needed the comfort of a friend just being there. Any time we face our own agony of goodbyes and we have to go it alone without loved ones or friends to wait with us, we stand in the goodbye that Jesus stood in when he agonized before his death.

In the garden Jesus feared the inner void and pain that would be his. As he walked forth from there, he began to experience this. He received a shattering blow: the kiss of recognition from Judas (Lk 22:47–48). It is the goodbye kiss of anyone who has been betrayed by the one they deeply love. It is a sledgehammer affront to the ego and it rips apart the trust of one's heart. Jesus stood there and received the hello of Judas which was, in reality, filled with goodbye and death.

Long before Jesus reached the hill of Calvary he was bruised and torn by much psychic and physical pain. He had been betrayed by one friend and denied by another. He had been brutally beaten and treated as an inhuman object. He had seen the desolate compassion on his mother's face as he passed her by on the road and he had heard the jeers and taunts of those who despised him as he was lifted onto the cross.

As Jesus hung there dying, he was most surely like 'the emptied one'. Beneath him stood his beloved mother and a handful of friends with heartache and sorrow written on their faces. All the rest of his friends were 'standing at a distance' (Lk 23:49). Inside him the ache of goodbye went deeper and deeper as he thirsted and pained and cried out in agony to his Father. But even his Father seemed distant. Jesus, in his weak, broken, helpless condition, 'cried out in a loud voice: "My God, my God, why have you deserted me?"' (Mt 27:46). This cry of the Beloved Son is the cry of every person who has known a devastating goodbye in his or her life, when the overpowering feeling of aloneness, emptiness, desolation, abandonment, fills the human spirit. It is the inner cry: 'Where are you, God, when I need you so much? Where are you? Why does this hurt so much? Why can't I feel your presence?' Jesus, the emptied one, bowed his head after a long, trailing lifetime of goodbyes and he surrendered to the deepest goodbye that anyone has ever known: 'In a loud voice he said, "Father, into your hands I commit my spirit." With these words he breathed his last' (Lk 23:46).

Stand strong in the resurrection

If we were left with Jesus' emptiness and desolation, if we had only our kinship with him in his goodbyes, it would not be enough to sustain us in our own leave-taking. We would draw comfort, but we would not have the hope of a future hello. The beauty of the paschal mystery, the mystery of passing over from death to life, of moving from goodbye to hello, is that it ends with hello. If Calvary is the deepest goodbye that anyone has ever known, then the resurrection is the greatest hello that anyone has ever proclaimed. The Father, the one whom Jesus treasured and with whom he yearned to be at home, surprised humanity and raised the Beloved from the dead.

Looking back on the resurrection experience, the disciples could say, 'Now we understand . . . this is the green of the wheat seed that has fallen on the ground and died' (Jn 12:24). This is the rejoicing that follows the mourning (Mt 5:5). This is the light after the darkness (Jn 8:12). This is the blessing of taking up the cross and following (Lk 9:18–27). Their understanding of the resurrection gave their world a different look. They could hold bread and notice how it was broken before it was shared; they could see the butterfly and remember the truth of a torn and empty chrysalis; they could awake in the morning, feeling the sunlight warm upon their faces and remember that dawn always follows the night. Jesus was transformed. His risen presence with them transformed their world. They were never the same again. The memory and reality of Jesus' death and resurrection had put the goodbye into perspective for them.

Jesus risen is a proclamation of 'hello'. He is a witness to us that when goodbyes do come we can grow through them. We can be changed, transformed. We can be raised from our empty places of loss and can experience something new within us. Jesus risen proclaims: 'Stay close to the Father when you suffer from goodbyes. Lean on this love and believe in his power to sustain you and to raise you from dark and lonely places.'

We must take our suffering and view it from the perspective of the resurrection. We must look upon our goodbyes from the direction of hello. We must stand strong in the resurrection, believing that there is something beyond death, there is something beyond pain and hurt and heartache. Here is where our strength and hope lie. This is the power of the resurrection at work in us.

Creative suffering

In Chapter 2 we reflected on 'the value of suffering'. Suffering in itself has no value. It is what we do with our suffering that makes the difference. The ministry of Jesus attests to this fact: He did all he could to alleviate the hurts of others. Yet, he also spoke of suffering as a source of growth, as a means of purification and inner conversion:

'I tell you most solemnly,
unless a wheat grain falls on the ground and dies,
it remains only a single grain;
but if it dies,

it yields a rich harvest.'   (Jn 12:24)

'Anyone who does not take up his cross and follow in
my footsteps is not worthy of me.'   (Mt 10:38)

'Happy those who mourn;
they shall be comforted.
Happy those who hunger and thirst for what is right;
they shall be satisfied. . . .
Happy those who are persecuted in the cause of right;
theirs is the kingdom of heaven.'   (Mt 5:5–6, 10)

Suffering can be beneficial when it leads to some kind of
'resurrection' in us, when a strength or a sleeping energy
in us is aroused, when talents so far unknown are recognized, when a clarity about life's purpose and direction
becomes keener for us, when a stronger sense of compassion for others deepens in us. There is so much within
us that needs to come to life. Moments of suffering, times
of goodbye, can cause us to peer inside our own tombs of
unfinishedness or incompleteness and we can discover
vast storehouses of resiliency, vitality, fidelity, love and
endurance.

In Chapter 2 we also explored the false notion that God
sends suffering to us in order to test us. God does not test
us, but the suffering that comes into our life because of
our human condition can sear our spirit in such a way
that we do become purer of heart, mellower, wiser, kinder,
more understanding or devoted or compassionate.
Extreme suffering of body or spirit can send a person to
deep inner recesses. It can be like the experience of a
refinery where the heat of the furnace of life burns away
the impurities. We can become like 'gold tested in fire' –
the best of who we are rises to the surface of our being.
This aspect of suffering is noted in 1 Pet 1:6–7:

You may for a short time have to bear being plagued by all sorts of trials; so that, when Jesus Christ is revealed, your faith will have been tested and proved like gold – only it is more precious than gold, which is corruptible even though it bear testing by fire.

The suffering of any goodbye, be it death or any other form of going away, can be a purification and a discipline in many ways. Things that we thought were important take on a totally different look: power or success or fame, to name a few. We learn the blessing of resiliency and the wonder of simple things taken for granted, like getting out of bed without pain or going through a day without a tremendous deadness in our spirit.

When our suffering refines us in such a way that it leads to an inner change or transformation that positively affects our life or that of others, it becomes *creative suffering*. Jesus suffered creatively. His emptiness led to a radical transformation of new life. His risen presence lifted the hearts of those who met him and changed their lives.

When we suffer creatively, when a part of what was dead in us is raised to life, when something of us is refined and made purer, we go, like the risen Jesus, 'to Galilee' (Mk 16:7). It is the Galilee of our own lives and we proclaim to others, mostly by our presence, that we have experienced hope and acceptance, that the emptiness and void within us have been filled with new life. We become enablers of life for ourselves and for others because there is something different about us and the way that we live. We have a changed perspective on life and we give others courage because we have been through a significant goodbye and have grown wiser and more tender. Many times those who have suffered creatively become active sources of comfort and consolation for others.

On a journey to St Louis I met a blind man. I shall never forget him. He greatly influenced my understanding of what it means to suffer creatively. He was a young, handsome man, wounded in Vietnam. He had spent his days since then helping blind college students cope with life, encouraging them to appreciate all the opportunities that were theirs and showing them how to live as an unsighted person. His enthusiasm for life was contagious. As he spoke, I felt I was in the presence of someone who had come through the fire and was pure gold. His appreciation of people and life was wonderful. As I walked off the plane in St Louis I knew that another seed of hope had been deeply planted in my heart by this messenger of God.

There are so many who have suffered creatively. They are the ones who walk in the footsteps of the risen Jesus. They carry the truth of resurrection in hearts which have been emptied and refilled. They know that farewells and goodbyes are not forever when one lives with faith in the eternal hello. People who have suffered creatively, who have taken their pain of body or spirit and are united with the emptied One who was raised from the dead, know that when a child grows up, when a friend moves away, when a loved one dies, it does not have to be the end. They believe that there will be growth, change, newness. They are grateful and rejoice in the love-bond that unites them with that child-now-grown, that friend moving on, that dying one coming into fullness of life. Their faith and their lives profess this belief: 'I think that what we suffer in this life [the goodbyes] can never be compared to the glory [the hello] as yet unrevealed which is waiting for us' (Rom 8:18).

Thus it is that whenever it is time for goodbyes, for

leaving behind and for moving on, I think of Jesus. I think of how many goodbyes he said, how many farewell tears he wiped away, how many hellos he walked into, how many risks of moving on he accepted. I think of Jesus, always travelling on in his years of ministry, stopping to catch his breath and his heart in mountain moments with the Father whose love was drawing him home. I think of Jesus, letting go, with a faithful belief in the pattern of hello-goodbye-hello. I think of Jesus, the emptied one, purely pilgrim 'with nowhere to lay his head', and I think of us, taking up and following.

Questions for reflection, integration, discussion

1 What do you consider to be the most difficult part of Jesus' journey of life?
2 When you reflect upon the life and message of Jesus, what is the most helpful aspect for you in facing your own farewells?
3 Where do you find hope in your goodbye times?
4 Have you known people who have suffered creatively? If yes, who are they and what are some of the characteristics of their growth in suffering?
5 Read/pray Chapters 14–17 of John's Gospel. Circle words in these chapters which seem to relate particularly to your own losses. What ideas, feelings, came to you as you read and prayed these chapters?

4

Like a flock of homesick cranes

Like a flock of homesick cranes flying night and day
back to their mountain nests, let all my life take its
voyage to its eternal home in one salutation to thee.

Rabindranath Tagore

What do homesick cranes have to do with goodbyes and
with the broken places of our lives? They are a symbol of
our inside, the place that I call the pilgrim heart. It is a
part of us that is never home, that is always stretching
and yearning to be home but knows that we have not yet
arrived. It is the yearning that was in Jesus, the broken
one, as he was drawn home to be with his Father, and his
winging homeward is a process that each one of us
experiences. It is the journey of our spirit and the road
markers along the way keep saying: HELLO this way,
GOODBYE that way. When we recognize this faith
dimension of our lives, it can make the necessity of goodbyes a little easier to understand and can help us to live
through the pain of our heartaches with more hope. We
can see our life experiences from the perspective of going
home, and we can know that the groaning and yearning
of our spirits is natural because we are in the homeward
process.

Because we are pilgrims whose homeland is not here,
we journey, search, travel, discover, live with mystery,

doubt and wonder. We see dreams come true; we see hopes alive. We see dreams dashed; we see hopes die. We start over again – with people, work, prayer, our whole life, all the days of our life. It is the way of the human spirit. Journey has become a very common word in the vocabulary of many people. It implies that we are going somewhere, that we are on the road travelling to a particular destination. In our mobile society, we take many journeys in our lifetime. Journey is also used in reference to the travelling that we do on the inside of ourselves, where there is a greater vastness and unfamiliarity than the physical continent far away from us.

The journey inside always has the aura of mystery and challenge because when we travel inward we can see only with the eye of faith. We must believe in the value of that inner road and trust that it will lead us to places in the heart that are waiting to bless us with their truth and beauty. It is much like exploring a mountain trail that one has never been on before. We walk along (sometimes huffing and puffing) and many times we pause and take another path or turn around and go back, thinking that the trail is either too ordinary or too hard or too long for us to continue. If we had just gone around the next bend and up the hill, we might have come to a magnificent vista of beauty. It is in this journey of the spirit that we enter into a pattern that is often repeated: we let go of the way we have known, we lose the way, we search for the way, and we find the way. We continually seek meaning in life and ponder the course of our inner direction. We keep counting upon facets of self-truth in us that we never knew existed. Our goodbyes can compel us to enter this pattern. They can lead us into deeper, newer territory if only we will continue, even when the going gets rough or the path seems unsure and we want to give up.

If we do choose to continue the journey inward, we can

never settle down in a newly found place for very long. These places are only temporary dwellings. They are havens of comfort, however, and they remind us that at the core of our being there is an eternal dwelling place of peace. But we must always move on because we are never finished, not as long as we are on this side of life. We are always in the process of getting there, of going home. If we are open and reflective as we continue the path inward, we keep discovering more and more inner vistas and places that we never knew existed. These are the markers toward peace. Sometimes when we discover them we say 'Ah!' for the beauty we have found; sometimes we exclaim 'Ouch!' in our pain of the truth; and sometimes we give a recognizing 'Oh!' for the depths to which we have come. These discoveries are signposts to continue on and we do so because we know that we are nomads who keep journeying, making our way through the hellos and the goodbyes of our travels. As we go along our way, we have tastes of our eternal home of everlasting peace, but these are brief, only appetizers. Sometimes we think that we are there, we feel so secure and so confident and so loving, but then life breaks all this loose and we find ourselves again searching for the meaning in life and yearning for peace. We realize once more that we are still far from home, that place of forever hello.

And where is the place of forever hello? It is the place of our own wholeness of self, that inner core of peace. It is also the place of being in the heart of God. The paradox is that when we enter the home of our God, we also enter the home of our true self. There is no more false self in us. We come home to ourselves in our wholeness, our goodness, our fullness of beauty. We know clearly and completely, for the first time, that we are truly made in the image and likeness of God.[1] The radiance of divine goodness blends and joins our own inner light and tranquillity and we know, in truth, that we are one. This homecoming is always in process. It is fulfilled in that meeting on the other side of life – eternity. But the deeper we go on our inward journey in this present life, the more we enter into the truth of this oneness. The greater our love of this God whose home is our own, the greater will be the yearning and longing in our hearts to be with God. We, too, will be the homesick cranes who are winging our way to the homeland. The goal will burn so brightly and deeply in the core of our beings that we will fly night and day back to our mountain nests, making our voyage with great expectation and longing.

Some of us are flying at great speed and intensity but some of us are still sitting in the marshland trying to find the courage to take off. The homesick crane in us knows that life is a journey, that we can never completely settle down and settle in, because 'home is the place we are always going to but never arrive'.[2] The homesick crane in us is the pilgrim who never arrives, who is always going home, sometimes not having any idea of which way to turn but knowing deep within that there is a goal awaiting and that it is well worth the journey with all its ups and downs, with all its hellos and goodbyes.

The tension that comes from this is that while we know that we are always going home, we must also be deeply rooted and involved in our present condition. We, like Jesus, must invest ourselves as totally as possible in loving others and in being loved by them. We must give ourselves to the human journey and not try to bypass it because it is in and through our humanness that we discover the beauty of the inner terrain. It is through this that we are transformed into who we are meant to be. It is through this that we unite with the heart of God.

In *The Problem of Pain,* C. S. Lewis stresses the longing for home in his chapter on heaven:

There have been times when I think we do not desire heaven but more often I find myself wondering whether, in our heart of hearts, we have ever desired anything else.[3]

The early Christians had a strong sense of this heaven within them. The author of the letter to the Hebrews fills chapter 11 with models of faith, people whose pilgrim-heart attitudes carried them through the difficult times of their lives. The fact that they believed their home was not here is made very clear:

> All these died in faith, before receiving any of the things that had been promised, but they saw them in the far distance and welcomed them, recognizing that they were only strangers and nomads on earth. People who use such terms about themselves make it quite plain they are in search of their real homeland. They can hardly have meant the country they came from, since they had the opportunity to go back to it, but in fact they were longing for a better homeland, their heavenly homeland.   Heb 11:13–16

The groaning within us

As we long for our heavenly homeland, as we yearn for a deep centre of peace in which to settle, we can feel within our spirits a groaning and an ache much like that of giving birth. For, as our pilgrim spirits mature, as they gestate and come into wholeness, they are filled with birth pangs, with the labour of letting go, with the struggle of new life which has been forming in us. The groaning within is especially intense when we experience certain forms of loss and brokenness. Adult transitions, confusion about who we are (particularly at mid-life), loss of deep relationships, desert prayer and darkness, harsh encounters with our false self or sinfulness, the pain of giftedness or creativity, all of these changes and challenges create a deep groaning in the human spirit, a crying out of the soul as one goes deeper.

This going deeper always involves a leaving behind. We cannot go deeper unless we let go of the place we have known. To descend into the depths of ourselves we must be willing to risk losing the security and the safety of that to which we have become so accustomed. It may mean leaving behind a certain self-image or some deeply-rooted concepts, such as our understanding of what it means to be family or friend, of what it means to be successful or whole.

When we are experiencing the groaning within us – those webs of confusion or disorientation or loss – when our life appears to be filled with failure and ungained dreams, when darkness looms up large against the tiny light of our hope, when our inner poverty gasps for a touch of fullness, when our brokenness cries out to be mended, it is then that our groaning is met with the Spirit of God who groans within us (Rom 8:18–23; 2 Cor 5:1–5). It is this God of life who blesses our inner birthing, standing by us, urging us to stay in the process, filling us with energy by the intimate touch of an eternal love shared with us.

All is on loan

What gives us the courage to stay with the groaning of our spirit? What keeps us winging our way homeward? How do we not clutch and cling to our securities and to all that we have come to know and to cherish? There is an ancient Aztec Indian prayer that reflects on the preciousness of life and the fleetingness of it. As the Aztecs thank the Creator for their life and breath, they acknowledge that they are only on loan to each other for a short while, and just like the drawings that they have made in crystalline obsidian fade, so, too, will their life quickly be gone.

Oh, *only for so short a while you have loaned us to each other,* because we take form in your act of drawing us.
And we take life in your painting us,
and we breathe in your singing us.
But only for so short a while have you loaned us to each other.

This 'on loan' philosophy is the first and most important attitude of a pilgrim heart. It can give us the courage to stay with the groaning of our spirit. It can carry us through many a hard time and can help us to hold our treasures in open hands when we want so much to resist the letting go of them. When we look upon all of life as being on loan to us, we look at it differently. We look at this loan for what it is – purely gift, given to us out of love. We reverence all that we have and take great joy in it, but we do not grasp, cling to, or hoard our treasures.

There is always a deep gratitude in those who look upon all of life as gift. As Isaiah 55 describes it, we do not earn what is given; it is simply there for us to receive and we do so in thanksgiving and in awe.

Oh, come to the water all you who are thirsty;
though you have no money, come!
Buy corn without money, and eat,
and, at no cost, wine and milk. . . .
Listen. Listen to me . . . and your soul will live.
(Isaiah 55:1–3)

Thus, we look at our world and its people through the eyes of a child caught up in wonder, and we approach it and care for it with all the commitment and tenderness of a responsible adult, knowing that it is only given to us for a time.

Deep down we know that all is on loan to us. Life does change and sometimes so quickly. Accidents happen, disease spreads, storms come, ageing continues, jobs terminate, mistakes occur. We go to bed one evening feeling good about life and ourselves. We awake in the morning and during the course of that day our world can be turned upside down by news of the death of a loved one, or an unexpected rift in a friendship, or the loss of a priceless possession, or a doctor's prognosis, or an unexpected financial decision. All of life is filled with loss and with letting go. For the one who believes that all is on loan, this is to be expected. Not that this expectation cripples the spirit of joy. Just the opposite is true; the present moment is treasured and enjoyed all the more because it is so precious and so fleeting. Those whose days have been numbered by an incurable illness will attest to this fact; suddenly the truth of life being on loan becomes a piercing reality and they are intensely aware of how fragile and beautiful it is.

Knowing this enables us not to fight so much when we are asked to let go, because we realize that those we cherish, while a wonderful blessing to us, cannot be kept from going home. The focus is on life and love, not on death and disaster, because the Christian pilgrim knows that the one thing that does last forever is love. It is joy, not sorrow, that Christian pilgrims carry in their hearts, because they know that they are on their way to their home in this God who is love.

Many times I have asked people in my classes to think about what they would pack in their 'suitcase of life' –

what the essentials were for them as they pilgrimaged through life. Doing this tells a lot about who and what one values in life. One of the most needed items that ought to be in our suitcase of life is courage. Pilgrims simply must take risks. Not to take risks keeps us from many experiences that lead to growth. Fear can keep us from going up that high hill to a vista of beauty and a whole new approach to existence. It can keep the birthing from happening in us. It can keep the emptiness from being filled.

Finally, the pilgrim heart learns to recognize and to cope with the demons along the way, those elements of life that pull us into the darkness, discouragement and self-pity. They can become so strong that we fall by the roadside and feel that we can never rise again. The demons which we encounter can eat away at our self-esteem, cause us to question our own goodness or the goodness of life, and create a great anxiety about the future. We lose hope of recovery, of moving on, and we think that we simply cannot do what is asked of us in our moment of goodbye. The journey just seems too much for us.

The Exodus in us

When pilgrim hearts are anxious and hurting from their journey and its struggles, it is sometimes difficult to name and to fight the demons along the way. I have often encouraged pilgrim hearts who were facing long stretches of inner wilderness filled with discouragement and doubt to read and to pray the book of Exodus. Many can identify with the journey of the Israelites as they moved out of their land of slavery, across the fearsome and harsh terrain of the desert, to the Promised Land – the movement from a place of non-freedom to a place of true freedom.

The pilgrim heart stands in a position similar to the Exodus travellers and knows that there will always be an Egypt that needs a goodbye. All these goodbyes call to us to not be held captive. Even though their life in Egypt was filled with brokenness, in many ways it was hard for the Israelites to accept the conditions for moving on. It meant leaving behind all that they had ever known and most of their possessions to face an unknown and uncertain passage which Deuteronomy calls the vast and terrible wilderness' (Dt 1:19). They left so quickly that they 'carried off their dough, still unleavened, on their shoulders, their kneading bowls wrapped in their cloaks' (Ex 12:34). So distraught and uprooted were they that later, when Moses shared God's promises of future freedom with them, they would not listen to him. It is difficult for anyone going through brokenness to feel and to believe that down the road all will be well, that God will provide. And because the feelings are not there, they often begin to lash out at life or to give up, as the Israelites did.

Secondly, it is easy to give in to grumbling on the journey. Over and over again the people of Israel brought their complaints to Moses: 'You have brought us to this wilderness to starve this whole company to death. . . . Why did you bring us out of Egypt? . . . Was it so that we should die of thirst?' And they 'put Yahweh to the test by saying: "Is Yahweh with us or not?"' (Ex 16:2–3; 17:3, 7). We often do the same when we go through our own wilderness. We won't let go of what we have known, what we are used to, so we miss the manna, the nourishment offered to us in our present condition. We ignore the treasure of friends, the power of prayer, the beauty of our own goodness, the hope of new life offered to us, or the truth that will set us free.

Yet another similarity in the Israelites' journey is that they had to take the roundabout way instead of the road that was nearest and most direct for them:

> When Pharaoh had let the people go, God did not let
> them take the road to the land of the Philistines,
> although that was the nearest way. God thought that
> the prospect of fighting would make the people lose
> heart and turn back to Egypt. Instead, God led the
> people by the roundabout way of the wilderness.
>
> (Ex 13:17)

As we journey along, we sometimes find that we are
caught in detours or side-roads of life that seem useless
or futile. But when we look back we see that the roundabout way was a valuable one. Although we never would
have chosen it, we have discovered deeper wisdom
because of this side-step on our journey.

Just as pilgrim hearts cannot settle down forever,
neither could the Israelites. They had camped at the Sea
of Reeds and found that it was a good, comfortable place.
Exodus 15:22 states that they wanted to stay there but
Moses pressed them to move on. This action is reaffirmed
in Deuteronomy: 'You have stayed long enough at this
mountain; move on from here. Continue on your journey'
(Dt 1:6). All of us have a basic need for security but if we
are on our way home then we, too, can never stay at our
cosy place when we are challenged by life to go forward
on the inner journey.

In noting the similarities of the Israelites' journey with
that of the pilgrim heart, the most strengthening and
hopeful aspect of the book of Exodus is the faithful, caring
presence of God with those who journeyed through the
wilderness. This truth is evident from the very first: 'God
heard their groaning . . . I am well aware of their sufferings' (Ex 2:23; 3:7). It is a truth that is repeated throughout the long journey. God constantly reassures them of

his strengthening and protective presence:

> 'I shall be with you . . . I have visited you . . .
> I will free you of the burdens . . .
> I will release you from slavery . . .
> I will adopt you as my own people,
> and I will be your God!'   (Ex 3:12, 16; 6:6–7)

Finally, just as pilgrims must recognize the demons along the way, so too must great attention be given to the messengers from God who encourage us and guide us. The Scriptures are filled with stories of magnificent carriers of God's word. In our day they are still strongly present among us. These messengers come most often in human form. They could be a best friend or a stranger on the street. They could be the voice of a child or the words penned in a letter by one who cares. These messengers may not know that they are carrying the word of God to us but they are. For God, in a great desire to comfort us, has moved within their beings and brought them to us in our wilderness of grief.

The attitude of a pilgrim heart will change the way we live through our times of Exodus and will help us to walk into the goodbyes that await us. We may still hurt deeply because, as Christian pilgrims, we give our hearts in love and choose to invest ourselves in life just as Jesus did; but we will approach the hurt in a different way. We will have hope that 'what we suffer in this life can never be compared to the glory, as yet unrevealed, which is waiting for us' (Rom 8:18). We will have courage to go on because we know that there is more to life than just what we have experienced here on earth. We will not be grasping for or clinging to people or things; there will be a deeper appreciation of them because we know that we do not own them but only have them for a time.

Whatever our present situation in life, we are Exodus people. Whether we are in Egypt, in the middle of the wilderness, or close to the Promised Land, whether we are engulfed in the grief process or are overjoyed with new life, whether we are in a painful or exciting process of self-discovery, whether we are coping with severe loss or are at a cosy place, we carry pilgrim hearts within us. This truth marks our lives with hello and goodbye.

Questions for reflection, integration, discussion

1. When have you most felt like 'a homesick crane'?
2. Are there any characteristics of a pilgrim heart that give you hope and encouragement? If so, which ones?
3. What would you pack in your suitcase of life?
4. What does the attitude of 'all is on loan' say to you about your present situation in life?
5. Which of the aspects of the Exodus most speak of your own pilgrim journey? It might be helpful to read or re-read the Book of Exodus, bearing in mind what we have observed in this chapter.

5

Praying our goodbyes

At every turn in the road a new illumining is needed
to find the way and a new kindling is needed to follow the way.   John S. Dunne

I remember so well the day I went to the home of a family
whose teenage daughter had been killed in a car accident. It was a moment full of deep sorrow and I knew that
it would be no easy visit. Helen took me to her daughter's
bedroom. There, on the bed, she had placed all of the
major mementos of her daughter's few and swift school
years. I remember especially the school jacket with a
bright, shiny medal she had won the day before she died.
Helen pointed out the mementos and spoke both proudly
and poignantly of her daughter's short but full life. We
stood there bonded in silent sadness, tears in our eyes
and hearts. Then we joined the other members of the
family and friends who had gathered. Each one who
entered the home was greeted in the same manner.

Now, many years later, as I reflect on that visit, I
realize what a beneficial ritual that was. It never occur-
red to me at the time that Helen was praying a goodbye;
but looking back on it, I see how she was doing exactly
that. Each time she escorted another visitor to the room
and stopped to ponder, she was living out the pain of her
daughter's death. The mementos of her daughter were

the images that Helen needed to link her with the child she had birthed, nurtured and deeply loved, the child she had swiftly lost in a blur of tragic time.

When we pray a goodbye our focus is on hurt and healing. Many times it is just a first step, or a beginning of the process of being healed. At other times it can be a very profound movement of healing in the heart of the one who grieves. It may feel like opening a window and airing a stuffy room, or like finding the key to a door that has long been closed. It may seem like finally discovering the right medication for a lengthy ailment.

There are four aspects of praying a goodbye: recognition, reflection, ritualization and reorientation. When we actually pray a goodbye the elements merge into one another and are not so easily separated as they are described later in this chapter. There may also be times when not all four aspects are present, but usually when we pause to bring our pain to prayer we can find them.

The four elements can be found in Helen's farewell to her daughter. Helen certainly *recognized* or named the deep pain of loss which came with her daughter's death. She used the mementos and the walk to the bedroom to *ritualize* that deep hurt. As she and her guests paused by the bed to *reflect* in silence, they began connecting the loss within them to the mystery of God and the human condition. The process of healing or *reorientation* was nurtured at that time. Helen was indeed praying her goodbye.

Prayer and the experience of goodbye

Since this experience of many years ago, I have grown in my perception of what prayer is and in my understanding of the grieving process. This has greatly influenced my approach. I now realize that prayer is so much more than 'talking to God' or reciting formal prayers or having good feelings about God. I have learned, too, that our prayer takes on a whole different look when we are experiencing the loss of someone or something highly significant in our lives. Grief has a way of plundering our prayer life, leaving us feeling immobile and empty. The experience of deep loss is that inner turn on the road of life of which John Dunne speaks. It is a time when we search for a light to find our way. We cry out for a 'new kindling' to burn within us so that we will have a desire and a reason to continue forward on the road of life.

All of us have those turns in the road. It is what we do or do not do with them that makes the difference. All too often we can let a life transition sit in our soul, discomfort us, empty us, discourage us and sometimes strangle us with its strong, clenching hold. Too often we can ignore a goodbye or fight it or push it away, but we do not get rid of the ache in this way. It keeps raising its voice inside us, at times when we least expect it. It drowns out the voice of joy in our life, bleeds our spirit of energy and enthusiasm; it destroys belief in our ability to rise from the ashes of our pain.

We need to acknowledge the ache of our goodbyes and to approach them in a way that leads to personal growth. When we pray a goodbye we do more than just pray *about* loss. Praying about it is to keep it out there, apart from us in some sense. When we truly pray a goodbye we enter into the whole matter; we live it. We connect our life with God and bring our pain into that intimate relationship, and know that the touch of God is the touch of healing. 'Power came out of him that cured them all' (Lk 6:19).

When we pray, we enter into a process of communicating with God, believing in our deepest being that this communication makes a difference in our lives. Good communication between persons always goes both ways – each listens and each responds. So, too, with God and us.

Sometimes we speak and sometimes we listen and sometimes there is a lot said without any words coming between the two of us. The wonder of our communion with God is that it can happen anywhere and anytime. Sometimes this event is as simple as seeing the morning star shine upon us and sensing a deep bonding with the magnificent Creator. Other times it is as deliberate as a structured meditation time, or as deep as a moment of intense, intimate silence. And sometimes it is as penetrating as the cry of agony which dwells in a heart full of pain. However it is that we communicate with God, and God with us, the truth is that God is deeply involved in our lives, touching us with love. This touch of God is the touch of transformation. We can never walk closely with God for very long and not have this presence make a difference in our lives, although we may not feel or see that difference for a long time.

It is one of the great ironies of our human condition that at the time when we most need to experience the tender compassion and strengthening comfort of our God, we very often feel a great distance in this relationship. The closeness or the sense of presence may not be felt. The desire and the energy to pray are gone. It is as though the human spirit has shrivelled up, gone dry and been swallowed in the darkness of heartache and the sawdust of sorrow. A tiny, weak voice in us calls us to pray but our tired, empty minds and hearts have no desire to respond. It takes us time to readjust to loss and change. It is much like plants that are moved from one environment to another; they are stunned for weeks, even months, before they respond to their new surroundings and begin to grow and bloom again. It may take the one in grief a long time before she or he feels like praying.

The psalmist echoed the emptiness of the people in exile with this lament: 'How could we sing a song to the

Lord in a foreign land?' (Ps 137:4, NAB). Indeed, it is difficult for anyone who feels alien from self, life, others, or God to sing a song to the Lord. Our prayer is greatly influenced by what our bodies and our spirits are experiencing. When we do not have a desire to pray, it does not mean that we have lost our faith or that we are being unfaithful to God or that God has forsaken us. Rather, it means that we are experiencing loss, and are at the bend in the road, feeling drained, hollow, empty, spent.

That is why our faith and prayer every single day is so important. It enables us to develop a strong union with God. We deepen our roots of love as we seek an ever more enduring communion in daily prayer. Then, when times of loss are weighing heavily on our hearts and we do not have a felt sense of God's presence, we can fall back on the steadfast belief that God always keeps vigil over us. 'Yahweh kept vigil to bring them out of the land of Egypt. . .' (Ex 12:42).

It is also very helpful during times of darkness and emptiness to have Scripture verses that are comforting and soothing to our aching spirit. These spiritual one-liners we discussed in Chapter 2 can help to carry us through the tough times. Some scriptural one-liners that are often balm to my woundedness are:

I know the plans I have in mind for you . . . plans for peace, not disaster, reserving a future full of hope for you.   (Jer 28:11)

I have loved you with an everlasting love.   (Jer 31:3)

Only goodness and kindness shall follow me, all the days of my life.   (Ps 23:6, NAB)

There is nothing I cannot master with the help of the
One who gives me strength.   (Phil 4:13)

I shall look for the lost one, bring back the stray, bandage the wounded and make the weak strong.
                                    (Ezek 34:6)

'Do not let your hearts be troubled.'   (Jn 14:1)

It is especially difficult to pray when very ill, particularly
if one has been receiving medication for pain. Remembered one-liners can be a comfort in great pain, but sometimes even this is not possible. A woman who had an
extensive hospital stay due to cancer surgery told me how
she just could not pray during those intense days. But
she took great solace in the fact that her community of
friends and family were praying, not just praying *for* her,
but praying in her place. 'How comforting,' she said to
me, 'to know that the community is at prayer even
though I cannot pray.' She surrendered in peace to this
fact and let go of her guilt and frustration in being unable
to turn her mind and heart to things of God. (Surely her
will to pray and her acceptance and joy of the community
at prayer were in themselves wonderful prayers of faith
and love.)

No matter how strong our faith, though, and no matter
how deep our love of God and others, there may be
moments (maybe days, months) in our grieving when it
feels like we just 'go through the motions' of prayer and
that all is aimless and worthless. But this is a very necessary part of our spiritual growth. It is the fallow time, the
wintertime, the barren time. It is the seedtime for us, the
dark of the earth before the greening, and we must continue to throw our empty selves into God's arms, leaning
on this stronghold, and trusting that the power of healing

is going on in us because this is the only way to springtime. God never leaves us during our winters of the heart.

When we want to give up God because we have lost our desire to pray and do not have a feeling of God's nearness, we need to remember that God understands us and accepts us in our sadness which is part of the human condition. At these times God says to us: 'Keep believing in the greening, in the springtime of your heart. I know that it feels as though I am far away from you but I am closer to you than your next breath. On your weary days, just come and sit by the well of life with me. I will stay with you. On your discouraged days, remember that I yearn to fill your life with joy. It will return to you in time. On days when you feel the ache will never go away, press your pain against me and know that I surround you with an everlasting love. Draw your strength and energy from me. I will sustain you in this wintry, dark time.'

How do we pray a goodbye?

One way we pray a goodbye is through the funeral or memorial service which the church wisely provides for those who grieve the death of a loved one. But funerals and memorial services are not enough. First, they do not provide for grieving the many other kinds of loss in our lives such as divorce or adult transition. Secondly, we need more than a one-time prayer to be healed of our loss. Grieving goes on long after the funeral is over. We need ongoing prayer to sustain us and heal us day by day.

The approach I have developed for praying our goodbyes is to use the four aspects I have already listed: recognition, reflection, ritualization and reorientation. The four parts of the process are developed in the following portions of this chapter and are used in the prayers of the final section of the book.

1. *Recognition*

We begin by identifying or naming the loss that we have experienced. We also name the hurt or pain that has been ours because of this experience. This is a moment of honesty for ourselves as we enter into the prayer process. It sounds simple enough to do, but some people walk around hurting for a long time before they identify their inner woundedness. Recently a woman in her 50s was feeling great restlessness and a deep anxiety about life. Eventually, she was able to name the loss she felt in the wake of taking early retirement. She went on to express a feeling of freedom and peace in knowing that this was a very natural response for her to have. Another woman shared with me her discovery of how stoical she had been about her father's death. She was the youngest in her family and had a close relationship with him. She had not realized how deeply she had buried her sadness because everyone else in her family appeared to be so strong in accepting the death. Once she acknowledged her gulf of grief she, too, knew she was free to take the next step in being healed of the hurt.

Naming the goodbye and the hurt may add to our pain initially because we see how real it is, but it is a necessary first step. In Chapter 1, I suggested some ways in which we might identify our goodbyes and name the hurts of our grieving. It might be helpful to return to that chapter when faced with the challenge of recognising or naming the pain of loss.

2. *Reflection*

The second step in praying a goodbye is one that our Western culture does not encourage and one which many adults need to develop on all levels of life: taking time to reflect. To give ourselves to reflection is to become comfortable with slowing down, with stillness, with solitude and aloneness, with not being afraid to look inward or to go deeper. In many ways our Western world says: 'Use all the time you have to keep busy, be successful and make money; do as much as you can as fast as you can; ignore the simple beauties in life and grab onto complexity; live for yourself and by all means, do everything you can to run away from and to avoid hurt of any kind. If you have to grieve, do it in a hurry and then get on with life.' Ours is a culture where life is lived on the surface, a life lived on the run with many fast food places to complement it. The inner world, the place of depth and meaning, the core of our being where God dwells, is all too easily missed or ignored. Because of this, many people have not disciplined their lives to include spaces of time where they do nothing except ponder, wonder, listen and be still.

This part of praying a goodbye can, then, be very difficult for those who are unaccustomed to taking time for reflection. They may be very uncomfortable with the quiet that it requires. Once they place themselves in this part of the process, however, it can be tremendously fruitful for them. In this second step, we take the hurt of the loss which we have identified, and we give it our full attention. We sit with it, look at it, face it, even though it grieves us to do so. One of the values of this prayerful reflection is that it enables us to discover our deeper feelings and to reconnect our lives with God. Sometimes we may be 'too nice' with God. We can hide our true feelings because we do not want to shock or offend God or have God think ill of us. We do not want to admit that we are capable of such feelings. We need to let God hear our cry and our distress. God knows it anyhow! Let God hear our anger and our confusions, our frustrations and our disorientation. Let God know that we wish things would change for us or that things were different. The people of Scripture have much to tell us about letting feelings out in the open with God. The author of Lamentations encourages:

Arise, cry out in the night,
  as the watches of the night begin;
pour out your heart like water
  in the presence of the Lord.   (Lam 2:19, NIV)

The psalms are filled with honest cries of grief and anguish:

How much longer must I endure grief in my soul,
and sorrow in my heart by day and by night? (Ps 13:2)

Be merciful to me, O LORD, for I am in distress;
  my eyes grow weak with sorrow,
  my soul and my body with grief.
My life is consumed by anguish
  and my years by groaning;
my strength fails because of my affliction,
  and my bones grow weak.   (Ps 31:9–10, NIV)

I am like water draining away,
  my bones are all disjointed,
my heart is like wax,
  melting inside me.   (Ps 22:14)

As we pour out our feelings to God in all honesty, we also need to listen. At first we may only hear our own hollowness and emptiness and dryness. Maybe we will feel swallowed up in our painful feelings and have to move away from prayer and forget the process for a while because it is just too much. But we need to keep coming back. Gradually we will learn to hear God's quiet, gentle, persistent, hopeful voice (cf. 1 Kgs 19:9–13). Many times a line from Scripture can suddenly become a powerful comfort or a guiding force for us. At other times a flicker of insight or a long-needed sense of hope or peace will come to visit us in a remembered line from a letter of a friend, or in the sound of the wind, or in the refrain from a song that echoes in our soul. Perhaps quite imperceptibly the truth of the ages about a God of love will come home to us. Slowly we will catch glimmers of hope, or peace, of understanding, or acceptance.

We may often walk away from our prayer time wondering if it was worth it, or if God was really there because we felt nothing or we felt only negative feelings. The secret is to be faithful to the quiet and the solitude, to continue to cry out to God and to make the attempt to be still in order to hear the truth. It is often in our poverty of spirit and our helplessness that we realize we cannot pray by our own efforts alone. It is God who comes to pray in us in our dark and sad moments (Rom 8:26). We are there, awaiting the blessing of hope. It is then that we understand the prayer of Ephesians: 'Glory be to him whose power, working in us, can do infinitely more than we can ask or imagine' (Eph 3:20).

3. Ritualization

As we become reflective and ponder the pain of our goodbye, we also need to ritualize it. Ritual includes two elements: a) the use of images or symbols and b) the use of some kind of *movement* in our prayer. With these two elements we thus act out some of the pain in us.

I discovered the value of ritualization as I acted out one of my own goodbyes. It was mid-November and I was hurting from the loss of a significant job change. After three months in my new ministry, I was still feeling the loneliness and vulnerability of a different place and a separation from good friends. Even though it was cold and windy, I went for a long walk. My heart felt heavy and my mind was as grey as the weather. Then I spied a milkweed plant along the roadside. I walked over and looked at its almost-empty seed pods. I felt bonded with them. They were being twirled away in the wind, and I knew that wherever they landed they would root and grow green there. I took one of the seed pods home with me and as I walked along the seed pods spoke to me of my need to let go, of the necessity of my investment in the present. I kept the seed pod in my office during the rest of that year and when the pain of letting go pounded on my inner door, I would look at the seed pod and gain strength from it. Every time I did so, I felt the strength to accept the present moment.

The milkweed pod was a means of connecting my prayer to my life experience. Ritual can do this for us. It is our life that we bring with us into our goodbye prayer. So we search for images or symbols that speak to us deep down at the centre of ourselves. Then we take our images or symbols and create some gesture of expression, some significant movement, out of which comes a connection with God, our self, and our life.

There are many images and symbols in Scripture which speak vividly of such things as loss, death, farewell, hope, strength, guidance, transition and transformation. The image of dry bones coming to life and dancing in the graveyard is a wonderful message of hope (Ezek 37). The images of fullness and harvest in the book of Ruth follow images of great emptiness at the beginning of that story. The compassionate shepherd bandaging the wounds of the sheep is given as a sign of God's care in Ezekiel (Ezek 34). The wilderness of the Exodus can remind us of our own inner and outer times of struggle and tough journeying. Jesus uses flowers and birds to caution against useless worry and anxiety, and a grain of wheat to speak of the transition that is possible only if one is willing to go through the dying part of life (Lk 12; Jn 12). These and many other images of Scripture speak to inner recesses of our beings.

Many of the common things of our life are also waiti. to speak to us of our pain and to connect us to the inner spaces where deeper meaning lies. There are innumerable ordinary images that can be used to call forth reflection on the hurt within us. Birds going south for another season can speak of the necessary transitions in life. Weeds pulled from the lawn or dustbins full of rubbish may remind us of the unwanted parts or our lives that we yearn to be rid of. Envelopes without letters, torn clothes or lost buttons, incomplete puzzles, empty anythings, all these can be signs of a process being unfinished. Ashes in the fireplace, dying plants or autumn leaves, empty nests, all these can be dimensions of the dying that life asks of us. The harshness of life can be seen in images such as uprooted trees, pieces of broken glass or torn paper. Shoes or suitcases might be a means of calling us to ponder our own inner or outer roads of travel.

There are also many common objects in life that can speak of new life and future hellos. Many times I have placed an object before a group and have asked them to connect their inner life with the object and the theme of the presentation. I am always amazed at the variety of valuable connections that people make. I have also asked participants to find an object that was an image of the goodbye or loss which they were currently experiencing. Once a man in his 40s brought a small chain as his struggle to break through his macho, unfeeling culture. A woman brought an empty nest before the group and spoke of her last child leaving home. A widow of just six months held up a butterfly sculpture and said that each time she looked at it, the silent message was that someday the pain of loss in her world would lessen. A young man struggling with how to use his gifts and talents shared how a little seed with a green shoot in it had been enough to encourage him to say yes to a new position which was scary and risky. The stories go on and on and so does the beauty found in images and their messages of healing.

Just as we can so easily take the use of images for granted, so too with the use of movement. In movement, we bring our bodies with us to prayer as we connect our hurt with the God of healing. It is the whole of our person which is at prayer. Movement or physical action helps us to put our whole self into the process. As with images, Scripture mentions many movements which ritualize the experience of goodbye and transition. There is the walk of the two on the road to Emmaus when they encounter Jesus and tell him the story of their downcast faces. It was in the carrying of the Ark of the Covenant that the Exodus people made their way through fear, discouragement and resentment to the Promised Land. Healing came in the washing of the leper, Naaman, in the river. There is ritual movement in the way Jesus touched the sick and in the jumping and dancing of the cripple made well in the Acts of the Apostles. The walk of the woman to the well and the hurrying back to tell the people of her inner healing ritualized her farewell to a sinful life.

Our everyday movement can also speak to us on a deeper level if we open ourselves up to them. Some movements or physical gestures that can help us to act out our grief are:

- sharing a meal with a friend as a love-bond with someone who nourishes us in our emptiness
- emptying a seed pod and realizing that we, too, have to let go before new growth can come
- lighting a candle to dispel our inner darkness
- emptying and cleaning cupboards or boxes while we are ridding ourselves of some inner clutter
- looking at photo albums when we need to remember the love and joy that past journeys have offered to us
- writing a letter in a lonely time as a reminder of connections of love that we still have.

Once I prayed the passion and death of Jesus by reflecting on the emotions of each event and I then used water colours to speak of the deep hurt that was there. As I painted the events, the colours cried out the pain to me and created an inner openness where I could connect some of my own pain with that of the Crucified One.

Another movement that is also a vital part of grieving and praying a goodbye is that of touch. Jesus could so easily have healed, and sometimes did, without the touch of his hand. But so often he stretched out his hands and the vibrancy of his being was power indeed for those who needed healing. Not long ago, a father spoke with me about the death of his son, aged 16. The father said it had been two years and his heart still hurt deeply whenever he remembered the tragic death. Yet, he said, the death of his son gave him something he had never had before: a recognition of how valuable the touch of another is. He told me how he had always been very withdrawn or reluctant when it came to touching others, even his own family. When his son died he felt the handclasps, the hugs and embraces from so many who cared and grieved with him, he realized for the first time what a powerful comfort and bonding an embrace can be.

We cannot pray the ache out of one another but we can bless it with the touch of our hands, the gift of our hug and our embrace. When we do this, we give the ache in the other permission to go on its way. Touch fills a person's being with the energy of bonding and love. Without ever saying a word, the message is given: 'I care for you. Here is some strength of mine to go on; here is some love to energize you now when you need it so much.' Touch connects one to another in care, makes contact with heartache, centres love, concentrates spiritual energies, warms the cold or exhausted spirit. Touch can penetrate barriers of despair, anguish, hardness or bitterness. A kiss on the cheek, a quiet embrace, arms linked or hands held are powerful movements in our ritualization of goodbyes. Let us not be afraid to risk this valuable aspect of praying our goodbyes.

4. Reorientation

Where does prayer enter into our use of these gestures and images? How does the God-connection happen? It happens in the midst of our reflection and our ritualizing. It is there that life is gradually reoriented or given a renewed direction and energy. God dwells within, at the centre and the core of our beings. When we use images, they connect our outer world to this inner world of our self where the divine dwells. This meeting is often an unspoken one. We sense it, but we do not always intellectualize it or have words for it. We connect with God much like the two from Emmaus connected with Jesus when their heartache on the road met the image of bread blessed and broken:

> Now while he [Jesus] was with them at table, he took the bread and said the blessing; then he broke it and handed it to them. And their eyes were opened and they recognized him; but he had vanished from their sight. Then they said to each other, 'Did not our hearts burn within us as he talked to us on the road and explained the scriptures to us?' (Luke 24:30–32)

As the two walked along and talked with Jesus they did not know they were being healed. It was in the breaking of the bread that reorientation took hold. 'Their eyes were opened,' i.e., they began to understand and to accept what their past experience meant to them. They regained the gift of hope and opened themselves to the healing which they needed.

When an empty seed pod calls to our heart 'Let go!'; or

when a newly-formed bud on a plum tree reminds us of hope, we are touching the space of our life where God dwells. It is our own Emmaus moment. Words from our heart to God's may follow the connection, but the connection itself can be a profound expression of our relationship to God. We are being reorientated, drawn into healing in a quiet sort of way.

Reorientation is a necessary element in praying our loss because this is where connections are made between our pain and the God of healing. It is where we bring faith to our grief. When we find some significance through our reflection and ritual, it gives us courage to go on. Many times I have looked at an image or have taken on some movement of farewell and have been blessed with an insight or a sense of meaning that was not there before. It reorientated my life.

One early summer I was out in the garden busily hoeing out the weeds that had decided to take over the patch. I didn't realize it but the garden had become a place of comfort for me as I prepared myself to move on to another ministry. I was finding it hard to leave a job, which I had created and developed, and place it in the hands and heart of someone new. On one particular morning I had a profound insight that was the beginning of great freedom for me. I saw the garden as my ministry, where I had planted and sown, where things had begun to grow. I saw that just as I would not be around to harvest its fruitfulness, neither would I be there to harvest the fruits of the ministry which I had begun. I remembered the words of Scripture: 'Neither the planter nor the waterer matters: only God, who makes things grow' (1 Cor 3:7). It was such a simple insight but it was the beginning of a cure for my heartache. Every day that I went to the garden from then on became a movement of farewell for me and a deliberate act of giving myself to the letting go process which I very much needed.

Yet another time I was out in the country on an autumn evening, going to visit friends on a farm. It was soon after the death of a dear friend and the pain of loss was still intense. As I walked along the pavement in the dusk, I heard the sound of geese flying south. I paused to be still and to listen. The sound of their southern flight filled me with tears of recognition. At the same time the strong image of geese in transition brought a twinge of hope to my heart. 'How much a part of life,' I thought, 'is this going-away thing. My friend's home is with you, God. I cannot keep wanting to have her here with me in the way she used to be.' I walked to the door that night with my first real acceptance of my friend's death. The ache returned many times, but each time it did I could recall the evening that I paused to pray goodbye as I heard the geese winging their way south.

One of the most poignant stories ever told to me was by a grandmother who related how her grandson had died of cot death. She told how her daughter and husband and their two children have since gone each year to the grave of the baby. On the baby's first birthday, they went to the winter cemetery and the children wrote 'Happy Birthday, James' in the unmarked snow. It was their message of love to their young brother who had died. It was their way of ritualizing some of the love and farewell that they continued to carry with them in their hearts.

God meets us at the bend in the road

Each of us needs to connect and to integrate our pain of goodbyes. If we enter the goodbye prayer of recognition, reflection and ritualization, the healing connections and reorientation can be there for us. The fragments of our lives will come together and life will begin to make sense again. Hope will return to our hearts. I believe this because I have known it myself and have known so many others who have experienced this reorientation. It has assured me that the God of healing is ever present with us and will never fail us. God, who is love and light, will be the illumination we need and will rekindle our hope as we meet that significant bend in our road of life. It is then that the images and words of Psalm 18 will take hold in our hearts and be the kindling for the future:

I love you, O LORD, my strength . . .
You, O LORD, keep my lamp burning;
 my God turns my darkness into light.

(Ps 18:1, 28, NIV)

Questions for reflection, integration, discussion

1 What prayer do you return to when times are tough? What is there about this particular prayer that draws you to pray it?
2 What image has most spoken to you about your experience of loss? How has it spoken to you?
3 Think of a time when you ritualized a goodbye experience. What did you do?
4 What Scripture passage would you use for praying your own present goodbye experience?
 What is the message in it that leads you to this choice?
5 Name a goodbye that you are currently experiencing. Review the aspects of praying a goodbye.
 How would you pray this particular one?
 (How would you identify it, reflect upon it, ritualize it?)

6

New melodies break forth from the heart

When we are in a grief process, the time comes for us in our goodbye experience to move on, to allow new melodies to break forth from our hearts. The time this takes is different for each person. What may take several years for one may take only a few months for another. We cannot compare because we are all such unique beings. But moving on must eventually be a part of our journey toward wholeness. Moving on is the time of coming back to life, of recovering our inner dynamism, enthusiasm and our desire to get on with the business of life. Moving on usually comes slowly. Days and months may go by, with a kind of plodding along, of just going on; some describe this time as existing or getting through, doing what you have to do. Occasionally, flickers of hope rush through our spirit like fireflies on a hushed summer's night. Briefly we feel good; we feel a bit of coming home to ourselves, and then the feeling is gone again. Slowly, though, we do come back to life; new country is revealed to us. A quiet resurrection happens in us. Finally, there arises in us the desire to move ahead. Life will never be as it once was because we are changed. The first green shoot has pushed its way through the dark soil.

The reality of moving on is this: we can never do so until we let go of whatever binds us to the past. If we have a heavy burden in our heart, it will drag behind us and create an ever-weary and ever-sad atmosphere in our spirit. If we have a memory that eats away at our integrity or an anger that gnaws at our peace, we will not move on in freedom. It will always be there to stir up negative feelings in us. If we have anything in us to which we hang on too tightly, anything that causes us distressful feelings, it will weaken our walking forward on the journey. It will sap our inner energy and mar our vision of where we are going and of how life is meant to be for us. We simply must come to a place in our lives where we agree to give up old securities which bind us, or painful memories which harm us, or dashed dreams which discourage us, or heartaching wounds which prevent us from discovering new dreams and from coming into fuller life.

I have learned about letting go, not just through books or ideas or from what others have told me about the need to do so, but from my own life experiences. I have discovered two very significant things: letting go never seems to get easy, and growth will not happen unless I can really surrender. Sadly enough, I have to keep relearning this because I like to hold on. Just when I think I have finally come to the full realization of how necessary it is to let go, I see that I am once again holding on to something too tightly and there I am again, not free to grow!

Often when I have spoken about the need of letting go, I can see confusion and concern in the eyes of the people present. Questions are raised: Does this mean that I shouldn't care any more? Should I stop praying for my daughter's marriage difficulties? Do I have to block out all the past from my memory of a loved one who's died? What happens to my own will and my responsibility if I let go? Am I supposed to be completely passive and allow others to harm me by their decisions?

To let go does not mean that we give up or that we do not care. Rather, it means that we choose to use our energies in another way, giving them another direction. Instead of concentrating on what has been hurtful, we look to what will be life-giving. We wish that life could have been otherwise or that things could be different. But it cannot be, so we accept that fact and move forward. We continue to care deeply but we also realize that we cannot change what is. All the struggling and grieving of our hearts will not bring back a loved one who has died, or erase a failure of ours, or keep a child from growing up or a parent from ageing.

To let go does not mean that we ignore old ragged and torn feelings and memories, or that we fail to recall the loved ones whom we miss so much. When these memories knock at the door of our consciousness, we open the door to see who is there and we acknowledge them. But we do not invite them in to spend the entire day with us.

To let go is to allow something or someone to be left behind in such a way that we are free to continue toward new country that is waiting to be revealed to us. It is to gain the freedom to proceed or to continue, to put behind us whatever has the power over us to influence our feelings, ideas, actions negatively. Letting go is an *attitude* that grows within us. It is never complete until it is acted upon.

Why is this action so hard to do? Why do we hang on so tightly? Perhaps because we fear not being in control or we fear insecurity. It is natural to want the known, the safe, the serene and the secure in our lives. Few of us like the feeling of uneasiness or uncomfortableness that change and letting go usually bring. We would rather cling to the present pain, the deadness, or the lack of life, than face what is foreign and unknown, no matter how good it is for us.

There are many different ways and times when letting go needs to be a part of us. We may need to let go of any of the following:

A person: This letting go may come through the death of a loved one, the termination of a friendship, a child going off to school or a son or daughter marrying. Life will never be the same as it was before those events took place. As we let go, we cherish the good memories and set aside the bad ones.

Unmet expectations: These can be expectations of ourselves, of our parents or of children, of friends or co-workers, perhaps of our church or our government. It can be extremely painful finally to accept a parent as he or she is, to see their flaws and weaknesses and to love them in their incompleteness. When a child so dearly loved continually makes poor choices and develops attitudes foreign to a parent's values, it can be a harsh and dreadful experience for a parent to let go of the child they hoped for and to accept the child that they have.

Dreams and goals: Especially at mid-life, but at any adult transition time, we come to 'truth times' when we see who we are and how we are. We can't be like someone else, or we won't be wealthy, or we will not be whatever it is that we thought we might be.

Old injuries of the heart: We all have them. They claim a lot of our energy at times. It may be the person who never liked us, or the one who destroyed us with jealousy or untruths, or the one who wiped us out with silence. It may be the relative who started the fight or the parent who abused us verbally or physically. We must also let go of our sinfulness. It is very hard to accept our own weaknesses or our failure and to trust in the mercy and forgiveness of God.

Old securities: Good health is a treasure. Sometimes we are forced to let go of it. Perhaps it is the natural ageing process of more wrinkles and less energy that we need to accept, or the inability to see well or to drive a car. We may lose it by a disease that slowly claims our body or a car accident that maims us in some way. There are internal treasures of which we also need to let go: consolations in our prayer life when the inevitable darkness and emptiness of spiritual growth comes; the hollowness and lethargy of depression that may take over the spirit; the ennui of mid-life that parks itself in the soul and seems as if it will stay forever. There are also those times when we are called upon to let go of the riches of friends who are close by, when a job promotion takes us far away and time or travel prohibit those regular conversations and enjoyable sharings that we once knew and valued so much.

Taking action

If we want to let go, we must first recognize what it is that needs letting go; then we need to accept the wisdom and the necessity of not clinging to it. Finally, we must gather up all the energy of our will that we possibly can and begin to take action – to actually leave the grief of our loss behind us. It is not easy to do this.

I have known numerous people who have let go and have come to the freedom to move on in their lives. One was a woman who always wanted her father to show love for her. He never did, not even on his deathbed when she expressed her love for him as he lay dying. All her life she rightly expected some sign of affection from this father who was verbally harsh and critical of her. After his death and after much grieving, she had to come to terms with how much power this man had over her life; even after his death she was still ruled by memories of his non-affection. Writing a letter of farewell to him began the process of truly letting go, and it eventually allowed her to express a truth she had never wanted to accept: 'My father will never tell me that he loves me.' Each time the memory of her father's lack of affection surfaced, she gently put it aside with 'That's all over now'. As she did this, her father had less and less power over her feelings and the sadness, guilt and distress that she felt so deeply were also being erased.

Surrender

Surrender walks hand in hand with letting go. To surrender is to give over to God, to give up our power over something that keeps us down or holds us back. When we surrender, we open ourselves up to the mystery of life, to the risks of the future, to the challenge of the unknown.

During our time of surrender, we especially need a personal relationship with a God whom we believe cares deeply for us. We need this because surrender demands that we trust God with our lives. We trust that we will not be harmed, that the letting go will be beneficial to our growth. How else can we take those giant, risky steps into unmarked territory? Surrender raises hard questions for us. Are we willing to trust God with our lives, our gifts, our treasures? Do we believe that we have the inner resilience to place ourselves in the hands of the future which we cannot see or name? Are we able to say with Ignatius of Loyola, 'Take, Lord, receive, all is yours now . . . give me only your love and your grace. These are enough for me'? Obviously a surrender of this depth requires a tremendous openness and trust of God with our lives. Few of us can pray this prayer with our entire beings, but all of us can pray it with at least a portion of our hearts.

For many of us it is scary to think of surrendering ourselves into the arms of God. 'What might happen?' is the secret question that pummels our thoughts. We do not yet fully believe that God is always, yes, *always* desiring our good and our happiness. We do not yet fully realize that God will be with us as a guiding power to love and to sustain us through whatever hardships and heartaches life may bring.

Surrender to God is a highly freeing event. It is like opening the lid of a jar and letting the butterfly wing away freely, or like a person paralysed for years being able to run and jump and dance again. It is the freedom of a bound Lazarus coming forth from the tomb.

Part of what keeps surrender from happening in us is our desire to be in control of everyone and everything. We want to make sure that it happens our way and in our time. And we all know that life is simply not that way, no matter how hard we try to work it out in our own control system. Much wisdom is needed to know when to be in charge and when to acknowledge our powerlessness and our inability to control all the events of our lives. We cannot just sit back and let everything happen to us. On the other hand, we cannot ignore the fact that there are aspects of our lives that we must let go of in order for us to grow.

Thus, to surrender is to have a willingness to be in another's hands, especially in God's hands, to be open to surprises and gifts we never dreamed possible. It is to hand over some of our own strong will to want to control everything, to let go of our own intense desire to make sure we never get hurt again. To surrender is to live with a mind and heart that is open to the future and to trust that all shall be well. When we let go and when we surrender, we are most surely on the pathway to healing.

Nature as a source of healing

One morning when I was in Israel I thought of how old wounds of goodbye rise up to haunt us. We were at

Megiddo and someone in the group had found pottery shards there – a little fragment of a handle, a small section with a design on it. They were reminders of a city long buried. I knew that shards came to the surface after a rain, particularly a hard rain. I thought of those old hurts in us, how they rise up like pottery shards from the earth to remind us of what is still there inside us. We are always in need of more healing.

Nature has been a wonderful source of healing for me. It is often through nature that I find the insight and the courage to let go, to surrender, to move on. The following are some insights that have blessed me with moments of healing when I was in desperate need of them:

Fireflies in the dusk: I was walking out a great loneliness in my life one night. As I moved along the wooded path, I saw a bright light in the distance. I quietly drew closer and saw that it was only one tiny firefly. It was just a small fragile frame that was giving forth such brightness! The lone firefly then joined the dance of a hundred fireflies as I walked in the late dusk. All across the vast meadow, far into the woods, their little lights danced and brought me a sense of bondedness. They were like a silent symphony, a gift to my lonely spirit. Like Christmas tree lights without the strings to mar their freedom, the fireflies held vigil with me. They danced for the earth, giving light to its darkness and I thought they danced for me, a pure and simple gift of beauty in the night.

In our darkest hour, it is often the smallest spark that brings us the gift of light, be it ever so frail a flicker. It is the moment of simple grace in a softly spoken word, a letter from a friend, an unexpected phone call, a warm touch from a loved one, or even a glance at the earth in its moment of hope. God has blessed our spirits with his own fireflies. They are small and fragile but they fly in our dark woods and their little beaming lights seem brilliant in our need.

Trees: Probably the most healing gifts of nature for me have been trees. I am rarely with trees for very long without a sense of blessedness or the truth of goodbye resting in my spirit. I once spent an autumn weekend with an oak tree. I watched the old oak with its wide-reaching arms give away his summer celebration. All night and all day the dead, brown leaves fluttered and flapped across the porch to the ground. Each little rap of wind tugged at the branches and lifted off another leaf. It seemed to me that the old oak tree stood ready and surrendered to the autumn event. I felt like an intruder on his farewell, seeing the wide open, stretched out limbs, the quiet, peaceful stance of his letting go. On that particular weekend the wisdom of surrender was rooted much more deeply in me.

The flight of geese: In the country place where I used to live I would often be awakened in the night by the sound of geese going south for the winter. It was a welcome sound that always left my heart feeling a bit sad and a bit glad. Geese speak to the part of me that knows transition and change are necessary, that leaving secure situations is an essential part of growth. When I hear flocks of geese call and see their patterned flight, they encourage me to allow myself to stretch and to grow. There is also a part of me that fills with nostalgia. My spirit cries out to them: 'Friends!' The flight of geese helps me to recall all the blessings that change and transition have meant for my own growth and all the special people who have walked through my heart because I have moved on. The migration of geese, and all birds, deepens the belief in me to keep travelling the inner roads when I would rather not go.

Frost: One winter morning I awoke to see magnificent lines of frost stretching across my window panes.

They seemed to rise with the sunshine and the bitter cold outside. They looked like little miracles that had been formed in the dark of night. I watched them in sheer amazement and marvelled that such beautiful forms could be born during such a winter-cold night. Yet, as I pondered them I thought of how life is so like that. We live our long, worn days in the shadows, in what often feels like barren, cold winter, so unaware of the miracles that are being created in our spirits. It takes the sudden daylight, some unexpected surprise of life, to cause our gaze to look upon a simple, stunning growth that has happened quietly inside us. Like frost designs on a winter window, they bring us beyond life's fragmentation and remind us that we are not nearly as lost as we thought we were, that all the time we thought we were dead inside, beautiful things were being born in us.

Kinship

Another valuable bonding is that which I have named 'kinship'. Kinship is not just another word for friendship, community or kinfolk. It may be all of those things combined and yet none of those things alone. Kinship is a rich bondedness that calls forth to the deepest part of ourselves. It is a mutuality of understanding, a sense of belonging, a union of spirits, a loving appreciation and a deep communion which comes from having known experiences similar to the person with whom we are bonded.

Kinship confirms our own journey and gives hope to our struggles. It encourages us to 'hang in there' when the going gets particularly difficult or overwhelming. Kinship nourishes us in our empty places and tells us that the dreams which we think we have lost have not died. When we experience kinship there is a mutuality of understanding on a mind and heart level. Something deep inside us connects profoundly with something deep inside the other. It is like recognizing a part of ourselves that we thought no one knew or could understand in such an accepting and knowing way.

Empathy and compassion are also a part of kinship. We can feel with the other and the other can feel with us. No words need be spoken. The solidarity of spirit is a loving resonance that speaks for itself. A union of spirits develops when one feels a value or a truth connected with the other who seems to walk some of the same inner footsteps of our own story of life. It is as if the vision in our own being meets the vision in another and something in us lights up in recognition, knowing that it is heard and accepted.

Kinship is deep communion that carries strength across many miles. We may not see each other often but we know and believe in the bondedness that exists. We draw strength from just knowing that the other is there and that she or he understands, that we can draw energy from one another in our time of need and return it just as generously when the time is called forth.

One day while reflecting on the Gospel scene of John 19:25–27, the truth about kinship in the midst of suffering came home to me. There beneath the cross of a dying Jesus were his dear ones caught up in the heartache of his pain: a mother hurting for her only son, a disciple grieving for his friend and teacher. There was a strong thread of bondedness among those wounded ones. In a great gift of kinship Jesus, even in his own agony, reached out and touched the hurt of others. He gave his mother to John and John to his mother, knowing it would comfort the ache in each one to have a home in the heart of the other. How deep their mutual love of Jesus was and what a bonding it must have been for them in their days of loss. A heavy hurt was experienced beneath that Good

Friday cross, yet the kinship that was shared helped them to withstand the cruel edge of death. We, too, stand beneath so many crosses where we hurt with loved ones who suffer. When we do so, God reaches into our ache and comforts us by giving us to each other in kinship just as Jesus did with Mary and the disciple, John.

This is what kinship is about: the gift of one to the other. It may be the kinship of a good friend, a friend whose heart is our second home, or it may be the kinship which we have with others because of a mutual experience which newly bonds us together in time of need. There are numerous support groups whose members feel a certain kinship — groups of recovering alcoholics or other substance abuse persons, families of cancer patients or those with other illnesses, parents who have lost a child through death or disappearance, men and women who are divorced or widowed, and many other groups whose members establish a bonding because of the understanding that connects them in their struggle. There is a strength in support groups which comes from the recognition that one's own process is normal and natural. One can look around the group and see others who are also trying to put the pieces of their lives back together again.

Kinship is not always easy. As we walk with others who are working through a loss, we may get very tired or impatient with their seemingly slow progress. We may become irritated with their self-orientation or their constant heavy heartedness or their strong hold on anger or breaking into tears at the most unpredictable times. It may take real effort to keep standing by them, but how necessary it is to do so. We need to be faithful. This is the gospel love which gives without expecting in return. We also need to extend invitations to growth, but when these invitations are not accepted we need not feel rebuffed or rejected. These refusals are simply indications that the grieving one is not yet ready to move on. Some day the time will be ripe and we will rejoice at our friend's new beginning. How easy it is for us to forget how long it took to go through our own goodbye moments and how patiently others stood by us. Kinship is grounded in the truth expressed in 2 Corinthians 1:3–4:

> Blessed be the God and Father of our Lord Jesus Christ, a gentle Father and the God of all consolation, who comforts us in all our sorrows, so that we can offer others, in their sorrows, the consolation that we have received from God ourselves.

Kinship is much needed for the healing of our woundedness. Our healing will be blessed by the consolation of understood pain and by a bondedness that supports us at times when we feel that the parts of our life will never reassemble into a whole again.

Recovering hope

Kinship encourages healing and with healing comes hope. When we are moving on from our painful goodbyes we have much in common with the Gospel stories of the resurrection. When Jesus was raised from the dead it was an event that seemed beyond the disciples' comprehension. The Gospels tell us that they were 'slow to believe' (Lk 24:25), that they doubted (Jn 20:25), that they 'did not believe' the hope of new life that was being proclaimed (Mk 16:11–15). 'The story seemed pure nonsense' to them (Lk 24:11). The disciples lived with incredulity and struggle before they finally accepted the truth that Jesus had been transformed. It was only after Pentecost that they fully understood, that they could look back on what had taken place and could feel within them a new surge of energy and vitality to walk into the future.

It is a natural piece of the inner process of healing that we come to the truth of our newness gradually, sometimes believing that we are on the mend and then getting discouraged or falling back into emptiness or desolation. But we do have our own pentecosts, those moments in life when we can look back and know that we have finally walked out of our goodbye. It no longer weighs us down all the time or constantly influences our thoughts and feelings. We feel a freshness about the days. We are glad to be alive. Deep within there is a tiny trickle of new life that doesn't stop flowing.

Love endures and goes on, in spite of all the feelings of grief inside us. Deep down we know that love can go with us beyond death of any kind, and we know, too, that time and the gift of God are wonderful healers of the heart. People who say that they won't love again, won't trust again, won't risk again, won't try again, are in the stage the disciples were in when they were overcome with the death of Jesus and walked dejected and downhearted, thinking their lives would never hold meaning and happiness again.

The human spirit is astounding in its resiliency and its ability to recover hope. That is what the resurrection proclaims: the possibility of transformation, the belief that we can be filled with new life, that the future will bless us.

Yet this I call to mind
  and therefore I have hope:
  Because of the LORD's great love we are not consumed,
  for his compassions never fail.
They are new every morning;
  great is your faithfulness.   (Lam 3:21–23, NIV)

Your sun will never set again,

and your moon will wane no more;
the LORD will be your everlasting light,
and your days of sorrow will end.   (Is 60:20, NIV)

Those who went sowing in tears
now sing as they reap.
They who went away, went away weeping,
carrying the seed;
they come back, come back singing,
carrying their sheaves.   (Ps 126:5–6)

We need to carry these promises of new life with us in our
hearts, especially when hope seems far from us.

Moving on

What can we do as we move on to new country, as we are
recovering hope and awaiting the melodies of new life to
sing in us? If we are attentive to the following, we will be
opening ourselves to the gift of our own spirit's resurrection:

- Be aware of your feelings and listen to what your inner
  world is saying.
- Accept what cannot be changed, be willing to let go.
- Be good to yourself by gifting yourself each day with
  little gestures of kindness (a talk with a friend, a walk
  with nature, listening to music, going fishing or play-
  ing tennis . . .).
- Open yourself to people; try to give yourself to just one
  helping situation, to gradually move out of your self-
  orientation.
- Keep leaning on God even when God seems far away.
- Trust in the power of God to restore you to health, to
  recover from your goodbye. Believe that God is a great
  strength.
- Keep returning to the truths in Scripture.

This book is about the goodbyes and how they happen in our lives and about what happens to us because of them. It is also a book about hellos. The pattern is unending: hello-goodbye-hello. It tells us of the seasons of our human journey. It proclaims that we do not need to stay lost or dormant forever. The 'homesick crane' in us does find joy in the journey. We do have periods in our lives when we wing our way with great energy and vibrancy. We do have seasons when we enjoy the delight and the adventure of life's travels, when we savour the taste of recovered hope and relish the vistas of new truths. There is new country waiting for us. There are new melodies that yearn to be sung in our spirits. We must believe this even on our most desolate of days. The season of springtime, of hello, awaits us all.

Somewhere within
the seed has sprouted.
I can feel its movement;
I can sense its energy.

Somewhere within
the rainfall has reached.
My desert is gone,
my dryness has disappeared.

Somewhere within
I've been given life again.
I can say goodbye to emptiness;
I can say hello to fullness.

Somewhere within
my yearning has been met.
The God of graciousness has graced,
the God of tenderness has blessed.

Somewhere within

I feel at home again.
I have enthusiasm;
I want to dream.

And so
the circle of my life-journey
has once more
come into its season of spring.

Questions for reflection, integration, discussion

1 What is the most difficult aspect for you in letting go and moving on?
2 What does kinship mean to you? Have you known this experience? If yes, with whom have you felt kinship and what was this like for you?
3 What Scripture passage most speaks to you about hope and hello?
4 Has there been a time in your life when you experienced a process of healing and of recovered hope? How did this happen?
5 As you look back over your reading of and reflection on this book what have been the most significant insights for you? How have these insights influenced the way you look at goodbyes and farewells?

7

Prayers for those experiencing goodbyes

Introduction

The prayers in this section are extensions of Chapter 5. They incorporate both images and movement focusing on many kinds of loss. These goodbye prayers can be turned to as various forms of loss are experienced in one's life. Most are for individual use, but any of the prayers could be adapted for use by a group.

These prayers are not meant to be the totality of praying a goodbye. They acknowledge the deep cutting truth of grief. They are meant to allow God's entrance into the inner rooms of our hurt and to move a bit further into beginning the healing process. Or they might be one of the significant, final gestures that bring to its conclusion the process of moving on.

Although writing is not always specifically suggested, it may prove helpful for you to have a journal or a notebook beside you when you pray. Before beginning your prayer time, reflect on the following questions and write whatever comes to mind:

- How am I feeling as I begin this prayer time?
- What am I hoping will happen in this prayer time? (For example, I hope I will draw some needed strength, deepen a sense of God's presence, come into further healing. . . .)

- How do I feel about my relationship with God?

It may also be helpful to write after the prayer experience: noting your feelings, insights, and deepened awareness. You may wish to end your time by writing a prayer.

As you begin your prayer time, first quieten your mind and your body. Become aware of how you are feeling physically. Take some deep breaths. Close your eyes. Just be still and rest in the arms of God for a few minutes.

I am suggesting that, for each of these prayers, you make use of a visual focus. Visual aids can become an excellent tool that enables us to connect our outer world with our inner world. Some people will find these particular suggestions helpful and meaningful. Others may find them less helpful, even intrusive. Give them a try. (You may be surprised to find just how helpful they are.) If they become binding or constricting in any way, lay them on one side, at least for the moment.

Several Scripture passages are also suggested providing the reader with alternatives for reading and/or meditation.

May these prayers be a source of strength and another step toward the hello which will come in its own time.

Prayer of one seeking shelter in the storms of life

Visual Focus: a candle burning

Opening prayer
Say the word *God* and let it pervade you... God's hands are around you; they shelter your life as a flame is sheltered in the storm.

Caryll Houselander

Pause to imagine God's hands around you; say the word *God* and let it fill your being with a sense of shelter and comfort.

Reflection

I know from experience:
standing deep within a linden tree
in a pouring summer rain shower,
one will not get wet.

I know from experience:
sitting very close under scrub oak
in a mountain downpour,
one will not get wet.

I know from experience:
when we draw very near to God's heart,
when we stand deep within God's shelter,
we will not be overcome
with the drenching pain of life.

Scripture

Then he [Jesus] got into the boat and his disciples
followed him. Without warning, a furious storm
came up on the lake, so that the waves swept over
the boat. But Jesus was sleeping. The disciples went
and woke him, saying, 'Lord, save us! We're going to
drown!'

He replied, 'You of little faith, why are you so
afraid?' Then he got up and rebuked the winds and
the waves, and it was completely calm.

The men were amazed and asked, 'What kind of
man is this? Even the winds and the waves obey
him!'   (Mt 8:23–27)

Meditation

Place yourself in the scene: the storm at sea. Imagine

that you are in the boat with Jesus. You move out into the deep waters. Gradually the sky darkens. The wind rises. The terror of the storm moves in with dark violence.

What are the sounds that you hear? What do you feel as you look into the face of the storm? How do you feel as the storm grows in fierceness and as the boat rocks precariously with the force of the wind and the waves?

Picture Jesus there in the boat. See how deeply he sleeps as the storm continues to rage. How do you feel about Jesus sleeping despite the distress that you are experiencing?

Go over to Jesus and wake him up. Speak to him. Tell him how you feel about the storm at sea. Then, tell him how you feel about the storm in your life now.

Listen to Jesus rebuke the wind and the waves. See him turn to you and place his hand on your heart as he tells the storm within you to be calm and to be still.

Invite Jesus to sit beside you. Notice the sky clearing to a deep blue and the sea growing calm. Experience the comfort and peace of the presence of Jesus beside you. As you do so, you may wish to repeat verse 12 of Psalm 2, quietly, slowly, allowing your heart to be at peace in the shelter of God:

Happy are all who take shelter in God.

Closing Prayer

God of my life, I am lost at sea; the wild winds and pelting rain of my troubles are threatening to submerge me in their power. I am tossed to and fro by the struggles that come upon me every day. There is so little energy in me to go on. I do not know how much longer I can hold on to hope. In my distress I cry out: Are you asleep in my boat of life? Do you care that I am battling the storm with every breath that I take?

Then your grace sweeps through my being and I remember the sacred voice of the ages:

If I flew to the point of sunrise,
or westward across the sea,
your hand would still be guiding me,
your right hand holding me.   (Ps 139:9–10)

All the truth of your sheltering love comes to comfort me in bits and pieces of the psalms: you do shelter me under your awning in times of trouble; you will hide me deep in the dwelling of your heart and protect me (cf. Ps 27:5). I know your love for me has been deep and strong since the moment of my conception for

you drew me out of the womb,
you entrusted me to my mother's breasts;
placed on your lap from my birth,
from my mother's womb you have been my God.
                                        (Ps 22:9–10)

So I beg of you, Comforting One who goes with me in the storm, look after me, I take shelter in you. Guard me like the pupil of your eye; hide me in the shadow of your wings, for I belong to you. I seek shelter, for you are my hope; you have always been my strength. I will rest in you, God, and trust that you will be with me no matter how great or how long or how intense this storm is. You are the source of my hope; with you for my strong support, my safety, I will make it through all this. Your arms are around me. They shelter me just as the flame of this candle before me is sheltered from the wind and keeps burning brightly. I entrust my life to you. Amen.

Prayer of one who feels broken apart

Visual Focus: broken pieces of a glass jar or paper torn into pieces

The following verses of Scripture are often used to portray the tremendous suffering and brokenness of Jesus on Calvary. They can also sum up the experience of those whose world has shattered, their once whole, peaceful lives strewn in pain. It is the image of those who feel their life can never be put back together again. If you are one of these brokenhearted ones, this could be your cry:

> For all my foes I am an object of reproach,
> a laughingstock to my neighbours,
> and a dread to my friends;
> they who see me abroad flee from me.
> I am forgotten like the unremembered dead;
> I am like a dish that is broken.   (Ps 31:11–13, NAB)

Prayer

Start your prayer time either by taking a sheet of paper and tearing it into shreds or by breaking a glass jar into pieces. In doing this you are expressing the pain and the harshness that you feel in your brokenness and that is causing you to cry out to God in your hurt. After breaking the glass or tearing the paper, the following reflections could be read.

Reflection

Jesus, your brokenness was real.
All the joy of being alive
all the beauty you saw in earthen things
all the people you knew and loved

118

all the satisfaction of healing
all the blessedness of your teachings
all the love you knew and shared
all of this – shattered on that hillside.
You were torn apart, broken, smashed.
All of life's joy seemingly destroyed,
terrible pain stretching out your agony.
Only a handful beneath your cross
to remind you of your wholeness,
and even this handful of loved ones
could not take your brokenness away.
You were a broken piece of pottery,
dashed against the stones of life,
a thing to be thrown away,
your flesh a ghastly thing to see,
your aching spirit a painful knowing.
On the cross that Calvary day
the sacred unity seemed torn apart.
Like a broken dish, like a broken dish,
you went to your grave.

Prayer

Picture your life as a pottery jar. See your life broken
apart. Look at all the pieces, harsh and jagged. Feel the
brokenness that is yours. Now gather the pieces together.
See yourself taking them to Jesus. Watch him hold the
pieces in his hands. Listen to him tell you about his
brokenness, how the Father raised him from the dead
and brought him to a wonderful wholeness. See the
pieces of pottery in Jesus' hands come together into a
beautiful jar. Take time just to gaze at the beauty of the
jar. Then open your hands and receive the jar in its
wholeness from Jesus. Pray your response.

Closing Prayer

Jesus, you were once broken apart. You know how it feels to be so shattered by the goodbyes of life. Help me to believe that I will one day experience wholeness again, that I will not have this terrible feeling of being torn into many pieces. Keep reminding me often that the Father raised you to new life, to a powerful wholeness that you had not known before. Encourage me to believe that, in time, I will no longer have this deep pain and hurt in my heart. I want to believe. Help my unbelief! Amen.

Prayer to regain one's inner strength

Visual Focus: the eagle

In the Bible the eagle is a symbol of strength and long life, a sign of blessing. The eagle is also seen as an image of God, carrying us, holding us up, protecting us like a young one is protected in the nest.

Picture yourself as the young eagle, helpless, needing to be fed, learning to fly. See how the parent eagle holds you up, encourages you, protects you. Then imagine yourself as an adult eagle with strong wings, flying in the sky.

Reading

Where do you get the strength to go on when you have used up all of your own strength? Where do you turn for patience when you have run out of patience, when you have been more patient for more years than anyone should be asked to be, and the end is nowhere in sight? I believe that God gives us strength and patience and hope, renewing our spiritual resources when they run dry (*When Bad Things Happen to Good People*, Harold S. Kushner)

Scripture Verses for Prayer

Phil 4:13	There is nothing I cannot master with the help of the One who gives me strength.
Is 40:31, NIV	Those who hope in the LORD will renew their strength.
	They will soar on wings like eagles
	they will run and not grow weary,
	they will walk and not be faint.
Ex 19:4	You yourselves have seen how I carried you on eagle's wings and brought you to myself.
Dt 32:11	Like an eagle watching its nest,

hovering over its young,
he spreads out his wings to hold him,
he supports him on his pinions.

Prayer of acceptance

Stand with arms widely outstretched on either side, in the fashion of eagles' wings. Lift up your head and receive the strength of God. Let it flow through you. Then let your arms fall at your side, take a comfortable position of standing, sitting or kneeling. Pray the following prayer:

God of strength, who calls forth eagles to bend wings in adoration, who sends forth eagles to wing wide in praise, I am in need of your strength. I am weary, tired, unable to soar in my sky of life. Carry me on your loving wings. Renew my strength. Give me the energy for the going and create in me an openness to future flying. Great God of eagles' hearts, I want to trust that you will bear me up, that you will support me. I look to you to renew my strength just as surely as eagles' wings are wide in the sky. Amen.

Prayer of farewell to one who is leaving

Visual Focus:
  Gather as a group and create a circle with your chairs.
Leader: Let's sit in silence for a few minutes, remembering the presence of our God who is with us and who understands the goodbye we are experiencing.
Prayer by leader: (after some minutes of silence) God of our life's journeys, we gather here to celebrate the goodness of and to ask your blessing as he (she) continues on the road of life. May the love that is in our hearts be a bond that unites us forever, wherever we may be. May the power of your presence bless this moment of our leave-taking.

Scripture: Acts 20:1–6; 26–38

Pause to recall some of the good qualities of the one who is leaving.

Then give each member of the group the opportunity to thank the one who is leaving for one or more of these beautiful qualities. For example: 'Thank you ____, for being such a good listener.' 'Thank you ____, for your sense of humour.' 'Thank you ____, for the gift of your generosity.'

Some members of the group might like to pray a spontaneous prayer for the person leaving. Or the group might like silently to hold the person leaving into God's love.

Closing Prayer: (Invite the group to join in this response after the leader prays.)

Response: We know that God goes with you.

Leader: As you journey onward, may you remember always that our love and appreciation for you are etched on our hearts . . .

Leader: As you experience the pain of change and the insecurity of moving on, may you also experience the blessing of inner growth . . .

Leader: As you meet the poor, the hurting, the stranger on your way, may you see in each one the face of Christ . . .

Leader: As you walk through the good times and the hard times, may you never lose sight of the shelter of God's loving arms . . .

Leader: As you question your decisions and wonder about the fruits of your choices, may the peace of God reign in your heart . . .

Leader: We praise and thank you, God of the journey, for our loved one who is soon to leave. We entrust _____ into your loving care, knowing that you are always the Faithful Traveller and Companion on our way. Shelter this loved one of ours and protect him (her) from all harm and all useless anxiety. May the future be a source of many enriching and transforming moments. Amen.

The leader then invites the group to join hands and to pray the Lord's Prayer.

At the end of the prayer time, each person in the group could trace the sign of the cross on the forehead of the one leaving as a sign of God's blessing and protection in the days to come.

Prayer of one who has been betrayed by another

Visual Focus: spittle on the face of Jesus

Find a quiet place where you can be alone. Begin by recalling the presence of God within you. Feel the strength of God's love flowing through your being. Picture God's hand in yours as you begin to tell the story of your hurt to him. Review the situation(s) of rejection and pour out your heart with all its thoughts and feelings to God who is listening very attentively to you.

Read and meditate

Mt 26:67   Then they spat in his face and hit him with their fists.

Mt 27:30   And they spat on him and took a reed and struck him on the head with it.

Is 60:6   I offered my back to those who struck me, my cheeks to those who tore at my beard; I did not cover my face against insult and spittle.

Mt 6:23   Someone who has dipped his hand in the dish with me will betray me.

Reflection

Jesus, I come to you,
overcome with revulsion
by the spittle on your face.
It slides down your cheeks,
it comes in the corner of your eye,
it sickens me, that sight.

I cry out in that ugliness.
I come to you, Jesus,
with cloth and water

to wipe away degradation,
to wash away the filth,
thrown from the bystanders.

You lower your head to my hand
and the slime comes on the cloth,
it hardly washes in water
so thick is it upon your face.
The touch of human defilement
clings to the creases of your cheek.

I have felt this painful deed
as I, too, have known rejection,
have heard, and hurt, with words,
thrown like spittle in my face.

I have felt marred and maimed in spirit
as my very person was cruelly rebuffed.
I have felt the slime and contempt
stick and press upon my life, too.

The recognition of my own pain and derision
almost overpowers my sad soul;
I stand stunned and sorrowful inside myself
I want to comfort you, Jesus;
I want to be comforted by you;

Jesus, spat upon and rejected,
have mercy on us all.

Meditation

Look at Jesus as he is spat upon and hit by others and
called names and jeered with cruelty. Hear, see and feel
the rejection. Look at Jesus reaching out to comfort you.
Feel him wipe the spittle from your face as you wipe it
away from his cheek. See him look at you with great love
and deep understanding.

Prayer to believe in your self-worth again and to open yourself to the possibility of loving and being loved:

Keep my heart open to loving others and to being loved by them, O God. Do not allow me to close off my life because of the scars of this painful rejection. Lead me into peace of heart. Help me to believe in my own goodness, so much so that I can reach out to others with confidence and receive their affection with trust. I pray for all those who have been brutally and harshly betrayed. . . and I pray for the one who has rejected me. Jesus, you continued to be a loving person even though you had been so painfully treated, please help me to be a loving person, too. Amen.

Prayer of one who is in constant physical pain

Visual Focus: your hand touching the hem of the robe of Jesus

Opening prayer

God of oneness, wholeness, I hurt and am in pain and I dream of a day when I no longer feel continual distress in my body. I cry out to you to hear me, to stretch your arms of compassion to me and to embrace me with your comfort. My being needs to be filled with your spiritual energy. I am weary with the struggle to feel well and to be in good health. It is so easy to slide into depression and self-pity, to be impatient and despondent. O God of the living, hear me. Fill my empty places with hope. Fill my life with a sense of joy in spite of this ceaseless pain. Help me to fight that giant oppressor of the spirit: discouragement. Remind me often of the good people in my life and of all the blessings that are mine as I struggle with this pain which is ever present to me. I praise and thank you for being a God who never leaves me.

Meditation

Read Luke 8:40–48, the story of the woman who had been ill for 12 years.

Picture yourself in the crowd. See Jesus there. See what a loving, kind person he is. Feel a drawing to him in your heart. Imagine yourself going to Jesus, leaning down, touching the hem of his garment. Feel the tremendous spiritual power that moves from Jesus into your whole body and soul. Hear Jesus ask: 'Who touched me?' See yourself stand up and speak to Jesus. Speak whatever comes to your mind and heart. Then listen to what

Jesus speaks to you. Perhaps he will tell you that you are being healed or that your pain can be a source of inner transformation, or maybe Jesus will tell you how you are to live with your pain. Perhaps he will speak no words to you at all, only look on you with a deep compassion and understanding.

Pray your response to Jesus.

Closing prayer (Psalm 18 – adapted)

I love you, Lord. I know you are my inner strength, especially now when my body does not have the strength that I took for granted in the past. O God, my deliverer, I turn to you. Sometimes I feel that I do not want to go on. I get swallowed up by the floods of self-pity and discouragement. In my distress I cry out to you. Reach out to me and rescue me from the enemy of pain. Set me free of its grasp of resentment. Fill me with courage. When the darkness of constant pain threatens to overcome me, brighten the darkness with your presence. With you by my side I can go through this. You are like a rock. You will be my strength. You are like a shield. You can protect my spirit from being broken by my body's pain. I will keep coming to you, touching the hem of your garment of love and feeling the spiritual energy which you share with me. I love you and I place my trust in you. Amen.

Prayer of one who is moving on

Visual Focus: a suitcase
(Place your suitcase in a position where you can see it during this prayer time.)

Read and pray: Psalm 121
The LORD will keep you from all harm –
  he will watch over your life;
The LORD will watch over your coming and going
  both now and for evermore.   (Ps 121:7–8)

Prayer

Guardian, guide, no pillar of cloud by day nor fire by night,
Yet I sense your presence with me, God of the journey.
You are walking with me into a new land.
You are guarding me in my vulnerable moment.
You are dwelling within me as I depart from here.
You are promising to be my peace as I face the struggles of distance from friends and security,
the planting of feet and heart in a strange place.

Renew in me a deep trust in you. Calm my anxiety.
As I reflect on my life I can clearly see
how you have been there in all of my comings.
You will always be with me in everything.
I do not know how I am being resettled,
but I place my life into the welcoming arms of your love.

Encircle my heart with your peace.
May your powerful presence run like a strong thread
through the fibres of my being. Amen.

Suitcase reflection
• What blessings of your life do you most want to carry

with you as you move on? Name these. (You may wish to write them.) Thank God for the gift to carry these blessings with you in your heart as you move on.

- What blessings are you most in need of as you continue your journey? Name these. (You may wish to write them.) Pray for the grace to have these as a part of your journey.
- If you wrote your blessings on paper, place these lists in your suitcase as a prayerful sign of your trust in God.

Closing prayer

(This litany is based on the prayer of praise, thanksgiving, sorrow and petition.)

I give you praise, God of my journey,
for the power of love, the discovery of friends, the truth of beauty
for the wonder of growth, the kindling of fidelity, the taste of transformation
for the miracle of life, the seed of my soul, the gift of becoming
for the taste of the little dyings which have strengthened me for this moment
for the mystery of journey, the bends in the road, the pauses that refresh
for the faith that lies deep enough to permeate discouragement and anxiety

I give you thanks, God of my journey,
for all I have learned from the life of Jesus of how to say goodbye
for those who have always stood near me and given me spiritual energy
for your strength on which I can lean and your grace by which I can grow

for the desire to continue on, for believing that your
  power works through me
for being able to love so deeply, so tenderly, so truly
for feeling my poorness, my emptiness, my powerlessness
for believing that you will care for me in my vulnerability

I ask forgiveness, God of my journey,
for holding on too tightly
for refusing to be open to new life
for fighting off the dying that's essential for growing
for insisting that I must be secure and serene
for ignoring your voice when you urged me to let go
for taking in all the goodness but being reluctant to
  share it
for doubting my inner beauty
for resisting the truth of my journey home to you

I beg assistance, God of my journey,
to accept that all of life is only on loan to me
to believe beyond this moment
to accept your courage when mine fails
to recognize the pilgrim part of my heart
to hold all of life in open hands
to treasure all that is gift and blessing
to look at the painful parts of my life and to grow through
  them
to allow your love to embrace me in the empty and lonely
  days
to receive the truth of your presence
to trust in the place of 'forever hello'

Prayer of one terminating a relationship

Visual Focus: a closed door

Sometimes we need to break a relationship, to bid someone or something farewell. It may be a marriage that has died, a friendship that is no longer healthy, a job that has failed, an old memory that has haunted us long enough and so on.

Acting out the goodbye

Find a private room in your home. Close the door tightly. Sit in front of the door, facing its closedness. Reflect on the person, or the job, or the situation, or the memory or feeling that you need to bid farewell.

Pray: Psalm 143 (adapted)
I sit here before this closed door
and beg of you to hear my prayer.
Hearken to my prayer.
Hearken to my pleading, faithful God.
You know how I have felt crushed,
hounded by this situation (or person) and how the old memories pursue me
like an enemy in the dark.

Lead me forth from the prison of my past.
It is time for me to let go,
to bid farewell, to walk away.
I feel as if I have been dwelling in the dark
for so long, like someone long ago dead and buried.

Hasten to help me, God of my life,
for I feel weak and lack so much courage.
I place my trust in you.
Show me the way in which to terminate
this part of my experience.

Rescue me from the enemy of my past, God,
for in you I place my hope.
May your Spirit guide me so that the coming days and
years of my journey will be ones in which I know
freedom, confidence and joy in the goodness of life.

After Psalm 143:
Write a brief letter of farewell to the person or situation
or memory which you are ending. Pray for freedom. Pray
for the one to whom you are writing the letter. (If praying
for an event or an experience, pray for those involved.)
Put the letter in your pocket. Open the closed door deliberately. Walk through it. Go outdoors, somewhere you
can continue to be alone. Walk in the woods or in the
country or along the beach or on the city streets. Find an
appropriate place to be alone. Pray. Carefully, slowly tear
the letter into small pieces as a sign of the break from the
relationship. Place the pieces in a rubbish bin or bury
them in an appropriate place. Return to your room. Leave
the door open as a sign of your new freedom and separation. Pray the following Scriptures.

Scripture

(Pray the entire psalm or passage suggested.)
Ps 146: The Lord sets captives free.
Ps 143: For the enemy pursues me.
2 Cor 4:7–18: Such an overwhelming power comes from
God and not from us.

Closing prayer

God of beginnings and of endings, grant that I might
have the strength to put an end to this matter which has
weighed so heavily on my heart and my mind. Grant that
I might bid farewell to this relationship which has

brought me so much pain and grief. You know that this dying which is so evident in the process of termination will truly be a step into new life for me. I feel fragile and frail at this moment, even though I know it is the right direction and decision for me. Help me to close the door on this section of my journey, to walk into new rooms of life. I need to experience a freshness and a vitality like the cool breeze of a spring morning coming through an open window. Be this vitality for me, God of compassion. Grant that I may turn my back and walk away from what has been. I pray that I may be healed of this hurt and I pray that any whom I have hurt through this experience may also be healed. Amen.

Prayer when a loved one has died

Visual Focus: a photo of the loved one

Take time to remember the special qualities which you so much valued and appreciated in your loved one's personality and life. Remember the special events in your lives that were full of joy and happiness. Offer thanks to God for all these blessings. Pour out your feelings of sadness and sorrow to God. Ask God to enter into the deep pain that permeates your life.

Prayer

'Father, I am coming to you!' (Jn 17:11).

Jesus, your departure was such an ache; your going away left a hollow in hearts, a tension between the love of your friends and the welcome awaiting you in going home to the Father. Such a mixture of feelings must have spun around in you: the sadness of your last farewell to friends and the anticipation of joy in the Father's welcome. You were leaving and sorely distressed. You were coming home and you were overjoyed.

Jesus, to the very end you lived our humanity, that life where one must always let go, must pass through death to enter into the fullness of life, that life where joy never completely buries sadness, where we move through days that demand goodbyes and come to moments that leave us no choice but to bid farewell to our loved ones.

Jesus, remind me in my own sad-heart time not to lose sight of the other side of ache, that glorious moment of happy homecoming, waiting for all of us in the loving hello of the Father. Send your Spirit to deepen my faith and to soften my sadness so that the vision of homecoming hopes will overpower the aches and struggles in all of life's farewells and goodbyes. Sustain me in this time and comfort me as I experience this great loss in my life. Amen.

Scripture

Is 25:1–10: The Sovereign Lord will destroy death forever! He will wipe away the tears from everyone's eyes . . . (v8 GNB)

1 Thes 4:13–18: We believe that Jesus died and rose again; and that it will be the same for all those who have died in Jesus; God will bring them with him.

Reflection

Take some time in silence (or with gentle music) to listen to your feelings. What are the strongest feelings within your spirit? Be as honest as you can with yourself. Don't ignore feelings that you do not like or want such as self-pity, guilt, anger . . . If you feel guilty, what has caused this in you? If you feel angry, what is there that is creating this feeling? After you have spent time allowing your feelings to surface, take each of your strongest ones and talk with God about them. Hold them before God and ask God to help you deal with them or to take them from you.

Prayer

I take my loved one by the hand and lead her (him) to you, God of love. Here is ____ (name). Accept my love and thanksgiving as I entrust her (him) into your loving care. I want ____ to be free to be at home with you. I ask that you save a place for me there beside her (him) and that you be my loving presence in all the lonely moments that await me. I ask that you fill me with motivation and energy in the days ahead when I feel like giving up; remind me often of my true homeland when I am caught up in the desolation of the journey. Help me to find joy in the people, events, and the beauty of nature which surround me.

Thank you for the gift of ____ in my life. I want to

believe that we will celebrate the treasure of our love again, when we are both in your presence forever. May this truth sustain me in the days to come. Take my sad and aching heart and comfort me. Comfort me, for I can only feel hollowness and emptiness. God of the sorrowing, draw near! Amen.

Prayer for trust when experiencing a loss

Visual Focus: open hands

Prayer

God of mystery, I turn my heart to you. I come before you in need of peace, grateful for the mystery of life and ever keenly aware of your promises of guidance and protection. I want to place my trust in you but my heart grows fearful and anxious. I forget so easily that you will be with me in all that I experience. Teach me to be patient with the transformation of my life and to be open to the change which I am now going through.

Reflection

Look at the geese of the sky: they neither worry nor are anxious about the winter warnings of their life, for they know within their deepest selves that their journey will take them to a place of shelter, of comfort, of nourishment, a place where winter harshness cannot reach them. See how they fly, winging homeward with sureness, with trust in their hearts' instinct. If these geese, who have not the faith and grace of human hearts, can follow the mystery and secrets of their deepest selves, cannot you, my loved and chosen ones, you whom I care for as my very own, cannot you be in touch with the mystery of your hearts? Cannot you trust in me to guide you on your journey of life? For I have promised to give you rest in seasons of tiredness, comfort in seasons of sorrow, peace in seasons of distress, strength in seasons of great weakness. Trust in me. Do not be afraid. I am with you. I will be your peace.

Scripture

'Peace I bequeath to you,
my own peace I give you,
a peace the world cannot give, this is my gift to you.
Do not let your hearts be troubled or afraid.' (Jn 14:27)'

After reading and reflecting on the Scripture verse, place your hands on your lap, palms up. Open them, ready to give and to receive from God. Sit quietly for several minutes in this posture of openness and trust. Pray for the gift of trust in God as you go through this experience of loss. Then read the following psalm verses:

The LORD is my strength and my shield;
    my heart trusts in him, and I am helped.
My heart leaps for joy
    and I will give thanks to him in song. (Ps 28:7, NIV)

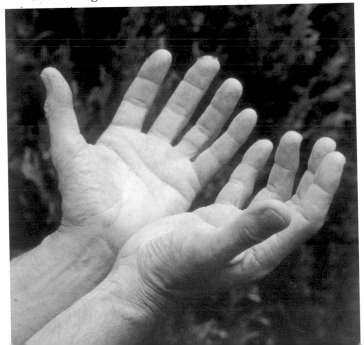

I am still confident of this: I will see the goodness of the
    Lord
  in the land of the living.
Wait for the Lord;
    be strong and take heart
    and wait for the Lord.   (Ps 27:13–14, NIV)

I, for my part, like an olive tree
growing in the house of God,
put my trust in God's love
forever and ever.   (Ps 52:8)

My God, my God, why have you deserted me?
How far from saving me, the words I groan!
I call all day, my God, but you never answer,
all night long I call and cannot rest.
Yet, Holy One, you
who make your home in the praises of Israel,
in you our ancestors put their trust,
they trusted you and you rescued them;
they called to you for help and they were saved;
they never trusted in you in vain.   (Ps 22:1–5)

Closing Prayer

God, in whom I trust, there is a part of me that is dying
and a part of me that is coming to life. I want to have an
open hands attitude towards you and towards my life,
but it is such a struggle to do so. Remind me often of the
peace which you extend to me. Thank you for your
beloved Son who suffered and gave me an example of
trusting in you. Renew me day by day. Encourage me so
that I may always be faithful to your call deep within my
heart. I open myself to the mystery of life and to your
love. Amen.

Prayer of parents whose child has died

Visual Focus: photos and mementos of the child who has died

> Arise, cry out in the night,
>   as the watches of the night begin;
> pour out your heart like water
>   in the presence of the LORD.
> Lift up your hands to him
>   for the lives of your children.   (Lam 2:19, NIV)

Sit quietly and look at the mementos of your child. Remember all that you loved about this child. Let the grief and sorrow in you come forth. Let it spill out and be laid bare. Share with one another the memories you most cherish about your child.

Scripture

Read Lamentations 3:1 24.

This is a lament, a cry of great distress and mourning, by one who is overcome with grief. The Hebrew people were not afraid to cry out their pain and anger. It was a step towards healing and consolation.

After the reading, pause and reflect: What do you cry out to God? (You may wish to share this with one another or write it in a letter to God.)

Litany of grief

(One spouse or family member reads the statement. The other(s) responds.)

Response to each statement: *God, be near to us, be our strength.*

We remember our lives, the way they were before our child died. How we yearn for those moments when all was well, when we looked forward to future growth together . . .

Every season will bring memories to us. Everywhere we turn we will recall the gift of our loved one. We will always remember the joys and the treasures of our dear one . . .

There will forever be an empty spot in our lives because we have lost our child. He (she) can never be replaced. We search for inner peace and we strain for a sense of acceptance of this reality . . .

Many feelings stir within us. We hurt with the heartache of our loss. Help us to believe that the sorrow will lessen as the days go on . . .

Our relationship with one another is influenced by this death of our child. It may be hard to share the terrible ache, to enter into the other's sorrow. Help us to share this heavy burden of loss. May our marriage grow stronger, not weaker; may our love deepen, not lessen, as we go through this grief together. . . .

(If other children in family)
The children who live with us need our attention and our love. May our grief over our child who has died not take away the love and affection which are so rightly theirs and which is so necessary for their own grieving time. . . .

We long for consolation and peace in our lives. We want to believe that our beloved child rests in the tender care of your loving arms, O God. Deepen the belief in us that our child is home with you. . . .

Reflection

Read John 19:25–27; 38–42. Quietly imagine Mary standing beneath the cross. Then see her with her dead son in her arms. Reflect on what her feelings, her thoughts must have been. How did she feel as she left Jesus in the tomb? Put yourself in Mary's place. See yourself as Mary and your child as Jesus.

Mary held Jesus all through her life. It was an embrace begun in joy, cradling him in her womb's world, then as a vulnerable infant resting warm against her breast. She fearfully drew him close as she fled into a foreign land; held him gratefully as she finally went home. She reached out and hugged him often all through those Nazareth years, binding up his childhood wounds and blessing his successes. She welcomed him in great relief as she found her lost one in the temple; and then kissed him farewell as he went to his ministry, and rejoiced in all the good that he did. Mary held her child again on that terrible day of darkness, with his wounded, ragged body stripped helplessly before all. She received him as a parent, into her arms of desolation. He who had been so welcomed now had to be left behind in a darkened tomb. Mary, on that day, wept with all the parents of the world who had lost a child so fresh with life and so fragile with the reckoning of the human condition.

Closing prayer (together)

We thank you, O God, for the gift of our ____ (name). You know what a treasure he (she) has been for us. It is not easy to part with him (her). The days are hard ones for us. The memories are there. Bless the hurt in our hearts as we trudge along through each day. Give us the energy we need to live our lives well. Do not allow us to move into bitterness and alienation with you or with one another. We can get through this painful time in our lives and we can go on with your strength to sustain us. Grant us peace. Amen.

Prayer of one who feels terribly poor inside

Visual Focus: anything empty (an empty cup, an empty seed pod, an empty box). Ponder the object before you. What does it say about your own emptiness?

Prayer

I do not feel that I have anything to offer to you, O God, or to anyone else for that matter. Inside me all is emptiness. I can only hear the echo of sadness. I am sitting in the ashes of desolation. I feel swallowed up in a sea of nothingness. Come, let me know the strong refrains of your love running through my inner pockets of poverty. At these times, when I feel so alone, so powerless, so sad and so desolate, the promise of your love does not enthuse me or hearten me. Take this empty spirit of mine, fill it with a deep belief in your abiding presence; allow me to bid farewell to whatever keeps me from relying on you. Help me to see that this emptiness can be a blessing because it puts my life in perspective and allows me to see you as the source of all inner energy and fullness. God of the poor, draw near to me in my need.

Scripture

1 Kgs 17:7–16: I have . . . only a handful of meal and a little oil in a jug.

Phil 2:5–11: He [Jesus] did not cling to his equality with God but emptied himself.

2 Cor 8:9: He became poor for your sake.

Reflection

'Poor in spirit'

What is this tiny whisper in me?
it weaves a voice of hope
through the poorness of my heart,
sifting, sorting, searching,
always finding many things
to call forth its cry: Thank you!

This tiny whisper in me
is the silent breath of faith,
stirred by a God, intimately near,
a God who has eyes, unlike mine,
who can see in the deepest corners
of pain, anguish, question, doubt;
who can recognize in all of this
elements of growth and goodness.

God of all stirrings in my heart,
see here, in this heart that is so poor,
the words of thanks formed in faith:
Thank you for all those life events
that I've fought and struggled with.

Thank you for all those surrenders
that seared and pained and burned;
thank you for the restlessness
that loomed up large against my soul.

Thank you for all that appeared to be empty,
for without those parts of my life
I would not be so poor in spirit,
nor nearly so ready to turn to you.

Closing prayer

God of the wandering ones, God of those who have so

little, from the chasm of my emptiness I draw out the meagreness of my prayer and I come to you. Everything is dry and fruitless inside me. All the richness of past consolations has disappeared. I feel void of even your presence and love. This time of experiencing my inner poverty is purifying and sometimes very discouraging. Your Word teaches that the poor in spirit are blessed, that these empty ones will inherit the kingdom of heaven (Mt 5:3). Is this poverty in my heart a part of that truth? Are you calling me to a deeper and fuller reliance upon you alone? Are you allowing me to be challenged in my spiritual journey so that I will choose where my treasure is, so that I will make more room for you in my heart? I still fight the empty days and nights; I still search for a prayer life that feels good; I still want to be perfect instead of loving myself with my flaws as well as my strengths. Will you teach me how to live with my inner emptiness? Will you enable me to let go of clutching and grasping after fullness? Draw me to your heart and bless me, your poor and needy servant. Amen.

Prayer of one who needs inner healing

Visual Focus: a plaster or bandage

Spend some time identifying what needs to be healed in you. (What is your hurt, your wound, your pain?)

Read Ezekiel 34:11–16
Pause to let the words of verse 16 rest in your soul:

'I shall look for the lost one, bring back the stray, bandage the wounded and make the weak strong.'

Prayer

God of love, you are the shepherd and I am one of your flock. The words of Ezekiel speak to me of your comforting presence and the truth of your care. I bear so much hurt inside from what has happened to me. My inner world has been one of anxiety and distress. In Ezekiel you promise never to let me out of your sight, to look after me and to keep me from harm. You assure me that you will rescue me when I am scattered, that you will draw me close when I lose my way in the mist and the darkness created by my wounds.

The pain of my hurts keeps me in a foreign land where I do not feel at home with myself or others. Help me to believe that you will lead me into a future rich with growth and peace. Show me where to rest, how to lay down my burdens and what to do in order to be healed.

Loving shepherd, I need to find a source of new life. Come, bandage my wounds and grant to this weak one a profound and deep strength to go on. Amen.

Scripture

Is 57:18–19: 'I will indeed heal.'

Is 35:1–10: The scorched earth becomes a lake,
    the parched land springs of water.
Is 58:6–11: 'Your wound will quickly be healed over.'

After reading and meditating on the Scriptures, carefully remove the bandage as a sign of your faith in God's healing power.

Closing prayer

Jesus, you cured those who were in need of healing (Lk 9:11). Take me by the hand as you did so many on your journeys, and help me to rise up. I need to walk with a renewed strength and vigour. Stretch out your hand and touch all within me that needs to be healed. The power which goes out from you can penetrate my being and cure what ails my spirit.

To the blindness in me you say: 'Shed the darkness. Look! See!' To whatever is withered, bent, crippled within me, you proclaim: 'Be freed! Go and walk your best in the world.' To the hunger in me for truth, beauty, peace, consolation, you promise: 'I will feed you.' To my distressed, disconnected, confused dimensions you say: 'I will bring you to your senses.' To the deaf and the unlistening parts of my heart you speak: 'Be opened!' To all that has died in me and needs to rise up, you call out: 'Come forth!'

I need your touch. I need your words. Jesus, healer, draw me to yourself. Amen.

Prayer of one who yearns for a new heart

Image: dry bones

Read Ezekiel 37:1–14

Imagine yourself as the dry bones. Feel the deadness, emptiness, void, or brokenness in your heart rise and grow into new life. See the bones coming together to form a person – you – alive, energized, renewed.

Prayer

Spirit of God, I feel too tired to go on, too empty even to want to be filled, too broken to put the pieces together again. Still, I feel a quiet stirring in me. It is the call to come back to life, to be energized and renewed. It is my heart crying out for newness, for a lighter spirit, for a keener sense of hope in the future.

Spirit of God, who draws together bones of the desert and dryness of the heart, come and take of my spirit all that has died in me. Dream in me again. Create of my brokenness a new and free heart. Draw together life in me. Let the dancing that's meant to be start its movement anew. The grace of freedom, the gesture of rebirth, all of this awaits me. I want to believe it in my depths.

Reflection

Listen to some of your favourite music. Let it fill your being with hope, with a sense of new life. Or, if you have a green plant, take the plant and touch the leaves. See the new life in it. Ponder the energy and vitality that flows through the plant.

Ezek 36:24–26: 'I will give you a new heart, and put a
 new spirit in you.' (NIV)
Is 43:18–21: 'See, I am doing a new thing.' (NIV)

Closing prayer

Create in me a pure heart, O God,
and renew a steadfast spirit within me (Ps 51:10, NIV).

These words come on the wings of the morning. They are
your quiet yet urgent messengers to me. For I do, indeed,
need a clean heart, O God. I need a heart that is free from
the dross of the past, a heart that is fresh with
enthusiasm and energy for the present as well as for the
future. A steadfast heart is what I want to claim, a heart
that does not waver about the truth or fall short when it
comes to loving well. Do not allow the events of the past
to dominate my memory or chain my heart to negative
feelings. Move me beyond this, God of new hearts. Fill my
entire being with a fresh freedom so that I will walk the
journey as well as possible. Create in me a vibrant spirit,
one that carries hope, one that believes in peace. Take
this heart of mine and fill it with your goodness. Amen.

Notes

Chapter 1
1. Kenneth Leech, *True Prayer: An Introduction to Christian Spirituality* (London: Sheldon Press, 1980), p 44.

Chapter 2
1. 'The Poems of Robert Frost', *The Modern Library* (New York: Henry Holt and Co., 1946), p 273.
2. Granger E. Westberg, *Good Grief* (Philadelphia: Fortress Press, 1962, 1972). Chapters 1–10 identify and explore many of the emotions associated with grief.
3. Gail Sheehy, *Pathfinders* (New York: Bantam Books, 1981), pp 383–428.
4. Harold S. Kushner, *When Bad Things Happen to Good People* (New York: Avon Books, 1981). See Chapter 3, 'God Leaves Us Room To Be Human', pp 72–86.
5. Donald P. McNeill, Douglas A. Morrison, Henri J.M. Nouwen, *Compassion* (London: Darton, Longman and Todd, 1982), p 40.
6. Harold S. Kushner, p 125.
7. Viktor E. Frankl, *Man's Search For Meaning* (London: Hodder & Stoughton, 1977), pp 123–124.

Chapter 4
1. Thomas Merton, *New Seeds of Contemplation* (New York: New Directions, 1972), pp 29–36.
2. Alla Bozarth-Campbell, *Life Is Goodbye, Life Is Hello: Grieving Well Through All Kinds Of Loss* (Minneapolis, MN: CompCare, 1982), p 89.
3. C.S. Lewis, *The Problem of Pain* (London: Geoffrey Bles, 1940), p 133.

Selected Bibliography

Batchelor, Mary. *Forty Plus* (Oxford: Lion Publishing, 1988).

Batchelor, Mary. *Meeting the Mid-Life Challenge* (Oxford: Lion Publishing, 1989).

Bauman, Harold. *Living Through Grief* (Oxford: Lion Publishing, 1989).

Brennan, Anne, and Brewi, Janice. *Midlife Directions* (New York: Paulist Press, 1985).

Chave-Jones, Myra. *Coping With Feelings* (Oxford: Lion Publishing, 1987).

Cole, Michael. *Going Home: What To Do When Somebody Dies* (Guildford: Highland Books, 1993).

Fischer, Kathleen R. *The Inner Rainbow: The Imagination in Christian Life* (New York: Paulist Press, 1983).

Fox, Matthew. *Original Blessing: A Primer in Creation Spirituality* (Santa Fe, NM: Bear and Co., 1983).

Frankl, Viktor. *Man's Search For Meaning* (London: Hodder & Stoughton, 1973).

John Paul II. 'The Christian Meaning of Human Suffering' (*Origins*, Vol. 13, No. 37, February 23, 1974).

Kubler-Ross, Elisabeth. *Living With Death and Dying* (New York: Macmillan, 1969).

Lewis, C.S. *A Grief Observed* (London: Faber, 1963).

Lewis, C.S. *The Problem of Pain* (London: Fount Paperbacks, 1962).

Lloyd-Jones, D.M. *Spiritual Depression: Its Causes and Cure* (London: Marshall Pickering, 1965).

McClung, Floyd. *The Father Heart of God* (Eastbourne: Kingsway Publications, 1985).

Nouwen, Henri. *In Memoriam* (Notre Dame: Ave Maria Press, 1980).

Rees-Larcombe, Jennifer. *Turning Point: Is There Hope*

for Broken Lives? (London: Hodder & Stoughton, 1994).

Sanders, J. Oswald. *Facing Loneliness: Starting Point of a New Journey* (Guildford: Highland Books, 1988).

Saunders, Cicely (ed.). *Beyond the Horizon: A Search for Meaning in Suffering* (London: Darton, Longman and Todd, 1990).

Smedes, Lewis B. *How Can It Be Alright When Everything Is All Wrong?* (San Francisco: Harper & Row, 1982).

Sturt, John and Agnes. *Created For Love* (Guildford: Eagle, 1994).

Sullender, R. Scott. *Grief and Growth: Pastoral Resources for Emotional and Spiritual Growth* (New York: Paulist Press, 1985).

Westermann, Claud. *Praise and Lament in the Psalms* (Edinburgh: T. & T. Clark, 1982).

Whitehead, Evelyn and James. *Christian Life Patterns* (New York: Doubleday, 1979).

Photographic credits

All photographs, with the exception of the photograph on page 46, are by Leonard Smith, Lens Ideas, Brantham, Manningtree, Essex CO11 1TB.

The picture on page 46 of the Judaean wilderness is by Jon Arnold Photography, 4 Summerhouse Close, Godalming, Surrey GU7 1PZ.